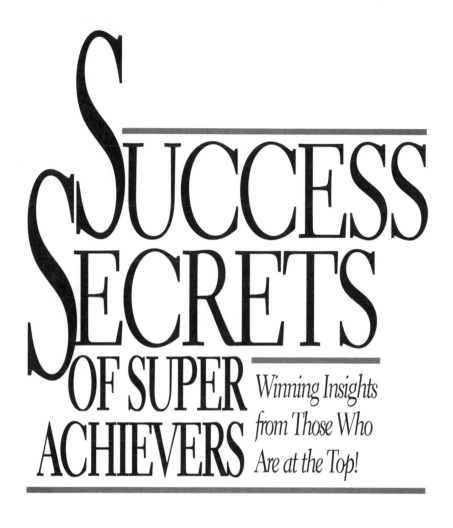

# SUCCESS SECRETS

## OF SUPER ACHIEVERS

*Winning Insights from Those Who Are at the Top!*

EXCLUSIVE TO

# JIM STOVALL

NARRATIVE TELEVISION NETWORK

*To my wife, Crystal,*
*for always believing in me,*
*to each of the special people who shared*
*a piece of themselves with me for this book,*
*and to Dorothy Thompson for helping me*
*put the pieces together.*

# $\mathcal{I}$NTRODUCTION

I want to compliment you for choosing and reading this book. Studies of Fortune 500 top executives reveal that one characteristic these leaders most often have in common is reading or listening to inspirational, motivational, and educational material on a regular basis.

Before I lost my eyesight, when I could read a book the way that you are reading this one, I am embarrassed to admit that I cannot honestly say I ever read an entire book cover to cover. After losing my sight, I discovered the Library for the Blind—a special program offering books on tape for blind and visually impaired people. This resource changed my life. I found that the greatest leaders of all time were waiting to share their secrets and wisdom with me if I would but take the time to listen.

I have now read the biographies of more than 1,500 great and famous people. One of the traits they have in common is a sense of expectation and destiny. They always believed that they were destined for greatness. I trust that *you* believe that *you* are destined for greatness, and that this book will be a launching pad for all that is yet to come.

Our society creates heroes in every endeavor of life. We all want people to look up to and emulate. And aren't we all intrigued by the lifestyles of the rich and famous, or of other individuals we admire? The purpose of *this* book, then, is to explore not just the "great lives of great people," but also great lives being lived by ordinary people who have great goals, vision, or passion. And beyond exploring these lives, this book is designed to help you explore your own life and determine which elements of *Success Secrets* apply to you.

One of the true joys of my vocation—and my avocation—is that I get to meet and learn from many of the best in every area of life. This book is the best of the best. It is not a compilation of other works but is, instead, a creative work containing many exclusive contributions given only for this book. A number of the thoughts, ideas, and concepts you will read here have never been shared before. I hope you will find it more than interesting, more than compelling, more than exciting. I hope you will find it life-changing and, in at least one of the nuggets of wisdom, I hope you will find the turning point you have been looking for.

There is a hunger today in our society for achievement and self-improvement. The result of this hunger is a glut of free and easy advice. Much of this advice comes from people who are in no way qualified to speak on achievement or self-improvement. Let me explain what I mean.

If you are traveling on a divided highway to the top of a mountain and you stop along the way to get directions or information about conditions up ahead, it is only logical that you would seek advice not from those on their way up the mountain, but from those who are returning. These are the people who have "been to the mountaintop." They know how to get there, they know how to stay there, and they know the pitfalls to avoid and the priorities that need to be set along the way.

*Success Secrets* provides exclusive advice from dozens of people who have "been to the mountaintop" in their selected field, and in life in general. For these people, success is not a theory or some type of abstraction; it is the way they have lived—and continue to live—their lives. Their advice is simple, straightforward, and effective, with no ulterior motive other than to help those who seriously want to join them on the mountaintop. Advice from common and mediocre people is plentiful, but these exclusive *Success Secrets* are rare indeed. And for those seeking their own personal greatness, they are priceless.

A wise man once said, "Don't ask for advice from anyone who doesn't have what you want." As you read this book, you will discover great people who *do* have what you want . . . and amazingly enough, these people are no different from you and me. In them, you will not see a different species of human being, but you *will* see the same doubts and fears that you face, and you *will* see their greatness and potential in yourself.

This book and the success secrets it contains should be your constant companion on the road to success. Don't try to reinvent the wheel. Simply follow the trail that has already been blazed, and you will find that your success is not a mystery, but a certainty.

# About the Author
## Jim Stovall

Despite failing eyesight and eventual blindness, Jim Stovall has been a national champion Olympic weightlifter, a successful investment broker, and an entrepreneur. He is the co-founder and president of the Narrative Television Network, which makes movies and television accessible for our nation's 13 million blind and visually impaired people and their families. Although NTN was originally designed for the blind and visually impaired, more than 60 percent of its nationwide audience is made up of fully sighted people who simply enjoy the programming.

Jim Stovall hosts the network's talk show, *NTN Showcase*. His guests have included Katharine Hepburn, Jack Lemmon, Carol Channing, Steve Allen, and Eddie Albert, as well as many others. The Narrative Television Network has received an Emmy Award and an International Film and Video Award, among its many industry honors.

NTN has grown to include more than 1,200 cable systems and broadcast stations, reaching more than 35 million homes in the United States. NTN also has an audience in 11 other countries.

Jim Stovall joined the ranks of John F. Kennedy, Orson Welles, Walt Disney, and Bill Clinton when he was selected as one of the "Ten Outstanding Young Americans" by the U.S. Junior Chamber of Commerce. He has been featured on *Good Morning America*, CNN, and in such publications as *Reader's Digest*, *TV Guide*, and *Time* magazine. His first book, entitled *You Don't Have To Be Blind To See*, was published in 1996.

# $C$ONTENTS

# Contents

# Contents

# JOHN AGAR

## "LEAD WITH PRIORITIES"

John Agar, an ex-U.S. Army sergeant-turned-actor, married Shirley Temple in 1945. Although their marriage ended a few years later, Agar's career as a leading man endured until the early 1960s. Long after the age when most actors retire, he continued to play bit parts.

Agar has been quoted as saying he is "poor but happy," and that statement can say volumes about a man's outlook on life and values, as well as his personal meaning of success and happiness. That view was reinforced in a letter he wrote to me in 1996 in which he stressed the following about success and his "recipe" for achieving happiness:

> "I believe love, honor, morals, and respect to all, including oneself, should be our top priorities."

# EDDIE ALBERT

## "PUT OTHERS FIRST"

I have had the privilege—on three separate occasions—to interview Eddie Albert: once via telephone, once in our studios in Washington, D.C., and the most memorable time for me, in 1995, when I interviewed him in California in a wonderful garden behind his home.

Many celebrities I have interviewed were difficult and hard to deal with. It's the kind of situation that almost makes you wish you had never met them, because they aren't always the person whose work you had enjoyed on screen. Eddie Albert, however, was everything I hoped he would be and more. I am proud to say that I consider him among my friends. He is a gracious individual. Let me give you an example.

When we arrived at his home for the interview, we had all of our luggage with us so we could go directly to the airport after the taping. When we had completed the interview, the crew was tearing down the equipment and packing up to leave . . . and Mr. Albert, then 87 years old, carried my suitcase to the front door. I was, in a way, shocked and embarrassed, but I told the crew afterwards that I wished we had footage of Eddie Albert carrying my suitcase!

Eddie Albert has sung lead with the San Francisco Opera and given critically-acclaimed performances of Shakespeare's work on the stage. He starred in many motion pictures and received an Academy Award nomination, but to most of us, he will always be Mr. Douglas, the city lawyer who found happiness (and frustration) on *Green Acres*.

During the interview, Mr. Albert had a refreshing way of looking at his work and his life. He said:

> **"I really don't care how I am remembered as long as I bring happiness and joy to people.**
>
> **"The most important thing to me is the relationship with my family, my long and successful marriage in a town and industry not known for long and successful marriages, and the friends I have developed in and out of the business who know they can trust my work."**

Few people know that Eddie Albert is a decorated hero of World War II. In a daring, courageous effort, he saved a lifeboat full of servicemen who otherwise surely would have perished. Once a year, every year, those servicemen that Eddie Albert saved put on a banquet to honor him. During my last interview with him, he had just returned from this annual event, and he was most proud of the fact that the men he had saved and the members of their families who attended the banquet now numbered more than 300 people.

Sometimes you do the right thing and it makes a difference . . . not only at that moment in time, but for generations to come.

# $S$TEVE $A$LLEN

## "IDENTIFY WITH THE AVERAGE GUY"

In 1995, I interviewed the legendary Steve Allen in his office at a Los Angeles studio. At that time, he was working on his thirty-second book and a new CD of original music. Few people know that, in addition to his work on television (as the creator and host of *The Tonight Show*) and his work as an author and a television and movie actor, Steve Allen is one of the most prolific songwriters who has ever lived. He has written more than 5,000 songs, and has a Grammy Award to his credit.

I remember arriving at his office that morning with a crew of six. We were told to set up in Mr. Allen's office for the interview. He was sitting at his desk, writing, when we came in. I asked if we would bother him with the noise and activity from the crew setting up. His assistant told me, "He won't even know you're here." During the half-hour of setup, Mr. Allen continued to work on his book and, when it was time to talk with me, he did a tremendous interview. One of the true secrets to Steve Allen's success, I feel, is his total focus on what he is doing at the moment.

During the interview, I asked him if there was one thing to which he would attribute his success. He said:

> "Whether it's a TV show, a movie, a book, an album, a personal appearance, or an interview like this, I never forget there's a guy at home who is my audience. He is my customer, and I try to come to him on his level and treat him as I would like to be treated. I have never considered myself a star, but instead, just the average guy's embodiment who works in show business.
>
> "I hope to give people the impression that if Steve Allen can do that, anyone can, because that is certainly the case."

Steve Allen has conquered every area of show business, and has been equally victorious in his personal life and in his battle with cancer. Because he lives to create, I know that we will be enjoying more of Mr. Allen's incredible creations for many years to come.

# DAVE ANDERSON

## "YOU'VE GOT A SPORTING CHANCE"

Dave Anderson has been a sportswriter for *The New York Times* since 1966. He has also written more than a dozen books, some in collaboration with such sports luminaries as John Madden, Frank Robinson, Sugar Ray Robinson, and Larry Czonka. So you might say that when it comes to observing and learning from the successes and failures of legendary achievers, Dave Anderson has had a courtside seat. And you might expect him to give pages of advice on how to make it to the top. Not so. Displaying his talent for choosing the right words (and not too many of them), this is what he wrote to me when I asked for his comments on success:

> "I don't pretend to tell people how to live their lives other than to do the right thing and work hard. Everything else should take care of itself."

Sometimes the simplest advice is the best.

# JOSEPH BARBERA

## "BE PERSISTENT"

Many of us can remember a time when "Saturday mornings" and "Hanna-Barbera" were synonymous. A generation of children sat glued to the TV set, giggling over the antics of Huckleberry Hound, Yogi Bear, Quick Draw McGraw, Top Cat, Magilla Gorilla, Tom and Jerry, and Scooby-Doo. Adults had their favorites, too, including *The Flintstones* and *The Jetsons*. Who do we have to thank for those timeless shows? Joseph Barbera and his business partner, William Hanna.

I am always intrigued by how people like Joseph Barbera got their start. When I wrote and asked him how it all began, he graciously sent me the following letter:

> "The first job I had was in a bank. At the time, the economy was so bad that I was fortunate to even have work. I didn't really enjoy being an assistant income tax man, so after work, I would create cartoons for magazines to keep myself

from going mad. Once a week, I'd go to the magazine offices to retrieve the rejects and then submit new cartoons. Eventually, I sold one, and after that, another. With that, I was off and running.

"Without persistence, it is impossible to experience success.

"Happiness is the real sense of fulfillment that comes from hard work. Winning Oscars brought me an amazing sense of reward, but when I attend gallery openings and see people wait in line around the block for me to sign an animation cel, it adds a joy that is indescribable. I feel fulfilled and honored when parents (at the signings) tell me they grew up on my cartoons, and that they enjoy watching them again 40 years later with their kids."

Keep on keeping on, as Joseph Barbera did. You never know what kind of success—and even more importantly, happiness—might be waiting just around the corner.

# DAVE BARRY

## "WHATEVER MAKES YOU HAPPY! (WITHIN REASON)"

You might say that Dave Barry has a unique way of looking at the world, a way of making the incongruities of daily life even more incongruous. Just ask the thousands of newspaper readers who have read his syndicated column. Or you might ask someone who has read one of his many books—with titles such as *Stay Fit and Healthy Until You're Dead* and *Claw Your Way to the Top*.

*The New York Times* once called him "the funniest man in America." He also received the Pulitzer Prize for Commentary. But success hasn't gone to his head—not even when the TV sitcom *Dave's World,* inspired by his writings, was on the air.

What does Dave Barry have to say about success? Let me share with you what he shared with me.

> **"I think success and happiness go together—if you do what makes you happy, you'll most likely be successful.**

"(Of course, you shouldn't do just *anything* that makes you happy; here I'm thinking of the Unabomber.)"

Vintage Dave Barry.

# $\mathcal{R}$ALPH $\mathcal{B}$ELLAMY

## "D O N ' T   B A C K   D O W N"

alph Bellamy holds the distinction of being honored with the highest awards that stage, screen, and television can offer. Some of you might remember him from the TV miniseries, *The Winds of War* and *War and Remembrance,* in which he played Franklin Delano Roosevelt. Or you might have seen him in one of his 107 movies. I had the chance to meet him many years ago.

When I first started interviewing movie stars for our programming on the Narrative Television Network, I was very intimidated, and most of the stars did very little to eliminate my fears. Ralph Bellamy, on the other hand, made me feel welcome and at home, and did everything possible to create a perfect interview. He made a career of being the second lead in movies, television shows, and on Broadway, and had developed the marvelous quality of making everyone around him look good and feel good. I will always remember and appreciate him for doing this for me during our time together.

Mr. Bellamy shared a story with me about his beginnings in show business. I think it applies to all of us.

"When I first started in the business, I had no talent, no contacts, and no prospects. My father was an accountant; he asked me to please join him in his business. I told him I wanted to be an actor, and I would never be happy unless I pursued my own goals.

"I remember when I got my first part in a play in Cedar Rapids, Iowa. I invited my father to come and see me in this play. As we were walking down the street to the theatre, we passed a rooming house with a sign in the window that said, 'Rooms Available. Absolutely No Dogs Or Actors.'

"My father pointed to the sign and said, 'Please join me as an accountant.' But he finally understood that being a happy actor is better than being a miserable accountant.

"A few years later, I had my own production company. My father's firm failed during the Depression, and I was very proud to have my father as the accountant for my production company for the rest of his career. He was a happy accountant and I was a happy actor."

And a successful one.

# *J*STAN AND *J*AN BERENSTAIN

## "FOLLOW THE GOLDEN RULE"

I f you've never heard of the Berenstain Bears, just go find the nearest available child. He will probably wonder what rock you've been living under, but don't let that put you off.

The Berenstain Bears are not just a multimillion-dollar corporation that has produced a series of popular children's books, TV specials, videos, and CD-ROMs. They are a way of life for creators Stan and Jan Berenstain. More than entertainment, the bears take on some of the problems that children face in everyday life (such as going to the dentist or moving to a new home) and show them how to cope.

When the Berenstains' two sons were youngsters, Stan and Jan decided to create "a funny family that would help kids learn to read. We chose bears because they can stand up and they look good in clothes and are fun to draw."

The Berenstains have been married for more than 50 years and, along the way, they have come to believe in and agree on some of the same important things. As Stan said in correspondence to me,

> **"We have faith in the eternal values, in being good, not being bad."**

That's the credo you'll find infused in every Berenstain Bears book. It's also a good rule to follow if you want to get ahead in life. You might call it one of the bare essentials!

# Jacqueline Bisset

## "Enjoy the Journey"

The British-born actress Jacqueline Bisset has never been in a blockbuster movie, but her name and her face are known around the world. Since her movie debut in 1965, her focus seems not to have been on commercial success, but on working when she chooses to and doing movies that interest her. At a time when many actresses clamor for attention with exercise videos, books, and products that they sell on the shopping channels, Miss Bisset appears to have chosen a less-congested path. I think that philosophy of a "simpler path" is reflected in her comments to me on success.

> "It is, for myself, very much involved with loyalty and a quiet mind. Sometimes loyalty to oneself, without the endless barrage of self-doubt that we beat ourselves up with, induces a feeling of peace and a realistic assessment of where one really is.

"To know that one is a good person, thoughtful to others, and not petty, is already a great success.

"To be responsible in one's given word to another.

"To stand up for good values without trying to control others by force and anger.

"Learning to listen openly to somebody without preparing your response before they have finished.

"Taking pleasure in the journey as well as the arrival.

"Not living in the future continually, or wishing your life away."

Success for most of us has less to do with how we look and sound, and more to do with setting and achieving goals. But as Miss Bisset points out, true success also involves treating others with respect, and living in the moment. We can't change yesterday. We can't see tomorrow. All we have is *now*. We should make the most of it.

# PAT BOONE

## "ACCENTUATE THE POSITIVE"

I interviewed Pat Boone one day at his office in Los Angeles. This is a man who has done so many things, and been around so long, sometimes we forget everything that he has done.

On the walls of his office are gold records, movie posters, Presidential commendations, and a history of the Boone family, showing that he is a descendant of Daniel Boone. It's a remarkable display that documents a remarkable career.

Pat Boone first caught the public eye on a 1950s TV show called the *Ted Mack Amateur Hour*. He wasn't an amateur for long. In addition to his work on television, he forged a successful recording career, appeared in several movies, formed his own record company, and authored a number of popular books. Like most celebrities, he's had his share of failures—some very public—but his faith has given him an anchor in the tough times.

Before our on-camera interview, Pat Boone spent more time talking about and asking about our work at NTN, and my books, than he spent discussing his own career. I have to say that he is one of the most genuine people I have ever met.

When I asked him what success means to him, he gave me just the kind of answer I would have expected.

> **"I define success as somehow having a positive effect on the lives of others.**
>
> **"That includes my own family. It includes my wife, my kids, my grandkids, my friends, the people that I'm associated with. In other words, if I'm involved in any kind of business thing, then I want it to be successful, of course, for those of us who have some major stake or investment in it. But I also want it to have some positive impact on the lives of other people.**
>
> **"So my Easter Seals work, and a number of other either humanitarian or just good old good-neighbor things, are to me as important as the initial career things that I do because it's all part of the same thing. One is sort of the facilitator of the other."**

If what you are doing with your life is hurting the ones you love, you will never be able to define yourself as a success. Do what Pat Boone does, and make sure that what you do "for the good of your career" is also good for the people around you.

# JIM BRADY

## "TAP YOUR HIDDEN STRENGTHS"

During an awards ceremony at the Kennedy Center in Washington, D.C., I had a brief opportunity to meet Jim Brady, a man who has a humility and sense of dignity that I have rarely seen in other people I have met. As you no doubt remember, Mr. Brady was the White House Press Secretary. He was with President Ronald Reagan in 1981 during a failed assassination attempt. The injuries he suffered placed him in a wheelchair. He went, in one instant, from the highest circles of power to a life-threatening condition.

Displaying a strength of character that few of us will ever know, Jim Brady chose not to ride off into the sunset. He chose not to disappear from view. Instead, he and his wife, Sarah, chose to bring something good out of this terrible event.

Jim Brady's life had been the American Dream come true. He grew up in a small town, got involved in politics, and wound up working with the most powerful man in the free world. He really had it all. But on the day he was shot, as they were taking him to the operating room, a neurosurgeon said, "I don't think he's going to make it." Three television networks took the doctor at his word and prematurely announced that Jim Brady was dead. But like a fighter who refuses to stay down for the count, he defied the odds and made a comeback.

The Bradys formed an organization called Handgun Control, whose watchword is ". . . working to keep handguns out of the wrong hands." Their tireless efforts on behalf of this cause have kept Jim Brady in the public eye, where he proves every day that where there's a will, there's a way.

As part of the therapy involved in his recovery, Jim Brady had to learn to use parts of his brain that most of us never bother to access. Imagine what the rest of us could do if we would follow his example!

When I wrote to ask Jim Brady for his comments for this book, he graciously sent me a copy of *his* book, *Thumbs Up*, and asked his assistant to respond to my questions. (His injuries make it difficult for him to express himself as he would like.) His assistant said,

> **"I feel his success in life comes from never giving up and from his sense of humor."**

If Jim Brady can fight on, and find reasons to laugh, I think we all can.

# Dave Brubeck

## "Making Good (and All That Jazz)"

In the music business, it pays to get an early start. Dave Brubeck's mother began teaching him the piano when he was four. He picked up the cello when he was nine. And all those years of training really paid off. By the time he was in his 30s, the jazz quartet that bore his name was a smash hit, and remained so for 16 years.

A prolific and original composer, Dave Brubeck is credited with making jazz popular at a time when it wasn't considered "cool." He and his group approached jazz from a different angle, and wound up creating a whole new kind of cool.

The letter that Mr. Brubeck wrote to me was brief, and had nothing to say about his music career. But it spoke volumes about the way he approaches life.

> "Success and happiness are two very personal conditions, defined in a very subjective way. Success is not always measured by recognition

or fame, nor happiness by material possessions and circumstances.

"For me, feeling successful and happy usually derives from the knowledge that my wife and six children are in good health and spiritually thriving. When these basic conditions exist, the secondary desires which affect our lives seem to materialize quite naturally.

"But when I, or those whom I love are at risk, a persistent faith that goes beyond human understanding must sustain me. That faith allows me to accept the unexplainable realities of our lives."

When your priorities are in order and your faith is strong, you won't have to go far to find success. It will find you.

# Oleg Cassini

## "A Design for Success"

It might appear that Oleg Cassini peaked early. He was, after all, named the principal designer for First Lady Jacqueline Kennedy in 1960. Decades later, however, he is still delighting customers with his unique designs.

Oleg Cassini had his first dress-designing success when he was 13 and living in Italy. He moved to the U.S. in 1936 but had trouble catching on in New York, so he moved to Hollywood and began designing costumes for the movie studios. He returned to New York in 1950, became a hit, and never looked back.

Many of the well-known people I've talked with have told me that their "secret" of success is something they read or heard elsewhere. Oleg Cassini is no exception. He found inspiration in the Rudyard Kipling poem *If*, and says he especially focused on the line I've highlighted. Let me share with you part of this great poem.

### IF

If you can keep your head when all about you
Are losing theirs and blaming it on you,

If you can trust yourself when all men doubt you,
  But make allowance for their doubting too;
If you can wait and not be tired by waiting,
  Or being lied about, don't deal in lies,
Or being hated, don't give way to hating,
  And yet don't look too good, nor talk too wise:

If you can dream—and not make dreams your master;
  If you can think—and not make thoughts your aim;
**If you can meet with Triumph and Disaster**
  **And treat those two impostors just the same . . .**

If you can talk with crowds and keep your virtue,
  Or walk with Kings—nor lose the common touch,
If neither foes nor loving friends can hurt you,
  If all men count with you, but none too much;
If you can fill the unforgiving minute
  With sixty seconds' worth of distance run,
Yours is the Earth and everything that's in it,
  And—which is more—you'll be a Man, my son!

# CAROL CHANNING

## "SAY 'HELLO!' TO HARD WORK"

In 1996, I interviewed Carol Channing during her worldwide tour with *Hello, Dolly!* She has done that role more than 25,000 times, but still brings an energy and an excitement to it that is totally unique in the theatre. She's a perfect example of why I enjoy Broadway theatre both in New York and as presented by the touring companies. I am very proud that here at NTN, through FM transmitters, we have opened the world of Broadway theatre to many blind and visually impaired people who otherwise might not have enjoyed this experience.

In all the years I've gone to the theatre, there was only one occasion when the audience gave a standing ovation in the middle of a performance. That was for Carol Channing in *Hello, Dolly!* When I asked her about this during our interview, she told me that it happened every night, and that she thought audiences did that for everyone.

What does a performer like Carol Channing have to teach us (besides maintaining unbridled enthusiasm)? This is what she said to me:

> "Just keep working—keep working wherever you are.

> "I truly live for my work, and I'm fortunate to have a family that understands that. My husband understands it, my son understands it, and the dog understands it. Just live for it."

Believe me: When you have that sort of attitude about your work, the world will STAND UP and take notice.

# JOHNNIE COCHRAN, JR.

## "BE PREPARED"

There is no doubt that Johnnie Cochran will always be best remembered as one of the lawyers who helped win an acquittal for O.J. Simpson. After that trial was over, however, he achieved a victory that brought him even more satisfaction. One of his clients, Elmer "Geronimo" Pratt, a man convicted of murder in 1972, was freed in 1997 after it was determined that he was wrongly accused. Twenty-five years of effort on this lawyer's part finally paid off.

Johnnie Cochran has been busier than ever since the Simpson verdict, writing a book and traveling around the country for speaking engagements. His first love (next to family), however, is and always has been the law. The key to his success? What he told me is, no doubt, the credo of his law firm.

**"Succinctly put, our three keys to success are PREPARATION, PREPARATION,**

**PREPARATION. Always remain focused, and never let anyone deter you from achieving your dreams."**

That's just the kind of summation you'd expect from a lawyer like Johnnie Cochran.

# RAY CONNIFF

## "YOU HAVE TO LOVE IT"

At a time when rock and roll music was making its biggest splash, composers like Ray Conniff were producing music that came to be described as "easy listening." He put out a series of successful albums that kept him in the public eye despite the shift to a new and different sound. But Ray Conniff actually began to make his mark long before that time, arranging music for the likes of 1940s "Big Band" leaders Artie Shaw and Harry James.

When a performer becomes a little less visible with the passing of years, you might think that his influence is no longer being felt. That's not the case with Ray Conniff. Let me tell you what he told me:

> "My daughter said the most valuable advice she ever got from me was one day over an espresso in our kitchen.
>
> "I told her that she should do what she loves to do the most, and not think about whether she got paid for it or not.

"That was what I did with my music. I used to write arrangements for bands just to hear them played, and went to sit in at jam sessions evenings in 'the village' of New York City just because I loved to play trombone.

"The result was that I eventually became very successful just doing what I loved to do.

"My daughter loves to write, and she is now doing quite well with a new, up-and-coming publishing company in New York City, so I guess [my advice] works."

I guess so? No, I *know* so.

# $C$HUCK $C$ONNORS

## "CONCENTRATE ON THE 'FUN'-DAMENTALS"

I had a chance to interview Chuck Connors several years ago, and I can tell you that he truly epitomizes the concept of "larger than life." His commanding presence on screen is not a trick of the cameras.

Few people realize that long before the days of Michael Jordan, Deion Sanders, and Bo Jackson, there was a two-sport athlete named Chuck Connors. He played professional baseball for the Los Angeles Dodgers and basketball for the Boston Celtics. While several athletes in recent times have tried to turn their success on the field or the court into success on the big screen, Chuck Connors never dreamed that baseball would provide the springboard for his jump into acting.

As we talked about how his acting career began, his recollections demonstrated a simple wisdom that I remember to this day.

> **"I was playing baseball in California. Becoming an actor was the farthest thing from my mind. I**

had had a really good year with the bat and was getting a lot of publicity.

"One of the studios called the team and asked about putting me in a small part, and I thought it would be a lot of fun. I was sure they wanted me to play a ballplayer. The next day, I showed up at the studio. Not only did they not want me to be a ballplayer—in my first scene, I was teamed up with Katharine Hepburn and Spencer Tracy!

"I remember asking Spencer how you do this, and he said that the key to acting is to 'show up on time, know your lines, and hit your mark. And never forget to have fun.'

"It took me a long time to get the first three, but from the first day on, I have always had fun."

We will always remember Chuck Connors for his starring role on television as *The Rifleman*. Let's also remember what he just told us about being punctual, prepared . . . and having fun.

# WILLIAM K. COORS

## "A LITTLE RAIN NEVER HURT ANYONE"

As president and chairman of the board of the Adolph Coors Company, brewery executive William K. Coors knows what it takes to run a large corporation. He has had his share of successes, but, like all of us, he knows the meaning of failure.

When he wrote to me with his comments for this book, he answered my question about success by referring back to my first book, *You Don't Have To Be Blind To See.* What he said was a validation of the work we do at the Narrative Television Network . . . and a recommendation that we focus not so much on ourselves and what makes *us* happy, but on what we can do to bring happiness to others.

> "To get a true understanding of what it means to be blind, everyone should wear a blindfold for a day. Sight is only one of our senses, and it is remarkable how a person who has lost the sense of sight, with proper help and

encouragement, can have the other senses compensate for that loss of sight. It is incumbent upon us as a society to provide that help and encouragement.

"To paraphrase a quote from the great Winston Churchill, 'Success and the happiness it brings is a matter of facing failure after failure with enthusiasm.' In other words, to fully enjoy life one must know how to enjoy the inevitable rainy days.

"The basis of our American society is that we all are created 'equal.' But it is difficult and not at all advisable to ignore the perception that some of us are more equal than others. To our good fortune, there is a rare benevolence common to our society that motivates us to iron out these inequalities."

To achieve the success you are dreaming of, you have to focus on the elements that will get you where you are going. But as William K. Coors would no doubt agree, success won't mean much if you can't find a way to ensure that others benefit from it, too.

# His Holiness, the Dalai Lama

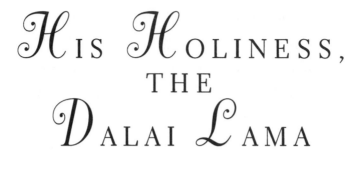

## "Develop Your Good Human Qualities"

As I was pulling together this book, I studied a number of entertainment, business, political, and religious leaders. I have to say that, at the beginning, I understood very little about the Dalai Lama. I still do not understand a great deal about his faith, but that's not what this book is about.

The Dalai Lama is a Tibetan religious leader. He won the Nobel Peace Prize in 1989 as a result of his appeals for nonviolent liberation of his homeland from Chinese rule. He has been in exile for several decades, but he continues to write and speak about his faith and his search for peace.

When I wrote to the Dalai Lama, I asked him the same question I asked everyone else: What are your thoughts on success and happiness? This is what he shared with me:

"We have all been born on this earth as part of one great human family. Whatever the superficial differences that distinguish us, each of us is just a human being like everyone else. We all desire happiness and do not want suffering. What is more, each of us has an equal right to pursue these goals.

"Because the very purpose of life is to be happy, it is important to discover what will bring about the greatest degree of happiness. Whether our experience is pleasant or miserable, it is either mental or physical. Generally, it is the mind that exerts the greatest influence on most of us. Therefore, we should devote our most serious efforts to bringing about mental peace. In my own limited experience, I have found that the greatest degree of inner tranquillity comes from the development of love and compassion . . .

"The more we care for the happiness of others, the greater is our own sense of well-being. Cultivating a close, warm-hearted feeling for others automatically puts the mind at ease. This helps remove whatever fears or insecurities we may have and gives us the strength to cope with any obstacles we encounter. It is the ultimate source of happiness in life.

"I believe that at every level of society, from the family up to international relations, the key to a happier and more successful world is the nurturing of compassion. We do not need to become religious, nor do we need to believe in an ideology. All that is necessary is for each of us to develop our good human qualities."

# DARREN DAULTON

## "YOU'RE ALWAYS WITHIN STRIKING DISTANCE OF SUCCESS"

Some baseball players are heroes to young boys who hope to make it to the major leagues someday. These youngsters want to play the game, but, if the truth be told, they also like the idea of getting their names on baseball cards!

What many children don't see is how difficult it is not just to make the team, but to stay there. Players who stay healthy throughout their careers, and who achieve a high level of success, are few and far between. Not every player can be a "superstar," and the ones who aren't have motivators that might surprise you.

Darren Daulton became a Philadelphia Phillie in 1980. He had to leave the game for a year in the mid-1990s because of an injury, and was with the Phillies until they traded him to the Florida Marlins midway through the 1997 season. He has been a National League All-Star, and was the league's runs-batted-in leader in 1992. When I wrote to ask him for his thoughts on success and happiness, this is what he had to say:

> "Out of all the accomplishments that I have ever achieved in life, the most rewarding is my personal relationship with Jesus Christ.
>
> "If you truly want a miracle performed in your life, ask Jesus Christ to forgive you of your sins, and hand Him the reins."

Some ballplayers might define success and happiness with Golden Glove Awards, batting crowns, or MVP trophies, but Darren Daulton has his sights set a little higher.

# MICHAEL DE BAKEY, M.D.

## "GETTING TO THE HEART OF SUCCESS"

D r. Michael DeBakey, one of the world's most eminent heart surgeons, was the first to complete a successful heart transplant in the U.S. He also pioneered numerous surgical procedures for the treatment of defects and diseases of the circulatory system.

An author and educator whose "firsts" in medicine have resulted in life-saving techniques, Dr. DeBakey has proven that if you love and believe in what you are doing, and you aren't afraid to try something new, you can have the kind of success that really means something.

Such a busy person should be hard to reach . . . but he responded to my letter less than a week after I mailed it. (Now, *that's* the kind of doctor we'd all like to have!) You might think that because of his profession, his chances of succeeding were greater. But as he says here, success is not a profession; it's the way we approach life.

"In my own lexicon, success is service to humanity.

"I was fortunate to have had parents who were models of virtue and to have had a profession that has been intellectually stimulating, psychologically fulfilling, and emotionally gratifying. The result is an exuberance unmatched by any accumulation of wealth, material possessions, or power.

"Real success requires respect for and faithfulness to the highest human values— honesty, integrity, self-discipline, dignity, compassion, humility, courage, personal responsibility, courtesy, and human service. These I learned early from my parents by word and example.

"Success is achievable without public recognition, and the world has many unsung heroes. The teacher who inspires you to pursue your education to your ultimate ability is a success. The parents who taught you the noblest human principles are a success. The coach who shows you the importance of teamwork is a success. The spiritual leader who instills in you spiritual values and faith is a success. The relatives, friends, and neighbors with whom you develop a reciprocal relationship of respect and support—they, too, are successes. The most menial workers can properly consider themselves successful if they perform their best and if the product of their work is of service to humanity.

"If, on the other hand, one measures success by public recognition, one may find that it is fleeting, lacking in inner satisfaction and tranquillity, and one may then feel disappointment at the fickle finger of fame.

"To achieve success, one must have a reasonable, commendable, and achievable goal and must pursue it with determination and dedication. If the goal is humanitarian, the joy will be all the greater."

# RICHARD M. DeVos

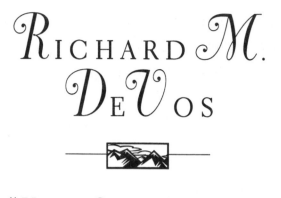

## "YOU CAN DO IT!"

Being a platform speaker myself, I always jump at every chance to hear the best speakers of our time. Richard DeVos is among the handful of great motivational speakers of all time.

There are a few people who have revolutionized a product, a company, or even an industry, but Richard DeVos has permanently changed the way that people do business around the world. As the leader of the Amway Corporation, he has a lot to teach us about finding success. This is what he shared with me:

> "I believe there are three key ingredients in the recipe for success. I call them the 'Three A's.'

> "The first 'A' is 'Atmosphere.' We need an encouraging atmosphere to achieve our potential. I had very little in the way of material

possessions growing up during the Depression, but I was fortunate to have a home with parents who expected me to do my best and work hard to achieve my goals. They never let me get away with saying, 'I can't,' because they knew I could.

"Thanks in large part to my parents, teachers, and other important people in my life who encouraged me, I was able to build a successful business that lets me spend my time encouraging others. When people ask me what I do for a living, I tell them I'm just a cheerleader.

"I travel around the world doing as my father taught me—to say to people, 'You can do it.' That's the message people really need to hear to succeed.

"The second 'A' is 'Attitude.' We must believe we can reach our goals, and we must be willing to look beyond obstacles to reach them.

"Long before my partner, Jay Van Andel, and I started Amway, we dreamed of owning our own business. Our friendship even began with a business arrangement—I paid Jay 25 cents a week for rides to and from school. We knew that when we found the right opportunity, there would be no stopping us from achieving our dream.

"The last 'A' is 'Action.' Without action, the other two 'A's' get us nowhere. We have to jump in and make our dream happen.

"It's easy to find reasons not to take action— lack of experience and lack of money are two common excuses. But with the right attitude and atmosphere, we can act despite these roadblocks.

"After World War II, Jay and I started our first businesses—a flying school and our community's first drive-in restaurant. We didn't know anything about either, but we figured that the best way to learn was by doing. We ran these successful businesses for several years before selling them to pursue our next opportunity.

"Our next business was selling Nutrilite vitamins person-to-person. We knew nothing about direct selling, and even less about vitamins, but we were willing to work hard to learn and to build this business. It was through our experiences with Nutrilite that we developed our plan for Amway.

" 'Action' also means persevering through setbacks and not giving up just because it would be the easiest thing to do. Jay and I certainly faced our share of problems—like people who thought that 'selling soap' would never amount to anything, and a fire that destroyed our factory in 1969. It would have been much easier just to let adversity win and get regular jobs like people thought we should. But we never even considered it. And 2.5 million Amway distributors are glad we acted on our dreams instead of our doubts.

"I consider myself very blessed to have experienced success. But what is most gratifying about success is the opportunity to help others. When we share our time, money, and experience to help others, we complete the circle of love that leads to our own personal happiness and success."

# PHYLLIS DILLER

## "MAKE UP YOUR MIND"

P hyllis Diller, a funny lady who, at the height of her success, probably inspired the term "bad hair day," blazed a trail that female comics have been following ever since. From performing for American soldiers in South Vietnam, to her work on stage, on television, on the radio, as an author, and as a recording artist, she has never been afraid to poke fun at herself. As a result, she has always given her audience the gift of laughter.

Do comics have a gene that the rest of us lack? Do they look at the world through Groucho Marx glasses? I wondered what Phyllis Diller would say when I asked her to talk about success.

> "Someone said: 'You are as happy as you decide to be.' I think it was Lincoln, or Woody Allen. I don't know. I know two blind men who never stop smiling: [jazz musician] George Shearing and Ray Charles. They bring happiness to millions of people.

"About success . . . there are many different ways to measure success. Gandhi only owned one sheet and he was a success. I know billionaires who are miserable and satiated and don't know a moment of happiness.

"It all boils down to spirit and thinking. Everything happens in the mind."

In Phyllis Diller's opinion, you are a success if you think you are a success. You can be happy if you decide to be happy. That means the ball is in *our* court.

# JACK ELAM

## "NO EXCUSES"

Jack Elam is one of those actors whose name might not always ring a bell, but his face always does. You might have seen him in *High Noon*, or *Gunfight at the O.K. Corral*, or in one of dozens of other westerns or crime dramas. Before he became an actor, he might have heard some discouraging words from the people around him; I don't know. What I do know is that his never-say-die attitude carried the day for him. Here's what he told me to say to you:

> "You can be assured that if a one-eyed, skinny kid with no special training or talent and no inside or outside help can make it by just trying and trying and trying . . . and taking chances . . . so can you!"

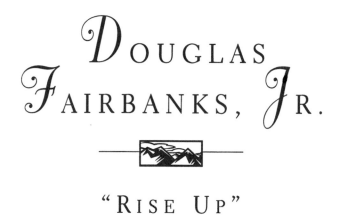

# DOUGLAS FAIRBANKS, JR.

## "RISE UP"

I will always remember the two occasions when I interviewed Douglas Fairbanks, Jr. No one embodies the classic Hollywood personality more than he does. And his father, Douglas Fairbanks, Sr., a standout in silent films, was a megastar in a way that simply does not exist today. Fairbanks, Sr., along with Mary Pickford and Charlie Chaplin, broke the stranglehold that the big studios had on the industry by forming their own studio, United Artists. This legacy of artistic freedom made it possible for Fairbanks, Jr., to blaze his own trail in the business.

Best known for his role in *The Prisoner of Zenda*, Mr. Fairbanks also appeared on stage and in numerous other films in the U.S. and England. He served with the U.S. Navy in World War II, produced more than 160 plays for television, wrote and published his autobiography, *Salad Days*, and took part in several public service missions for the U.S., including a mission to Latin

America in the 1940s as a Presidential envoy. He grew up surrounded by some of the biggest names in entertainment, business, and politics, and yet he became and remained a gracious and humble man who never lost himself amid the tinsel and footlights.

During one of our interviews, he reflected on his life and expressed satisfaction with his achievements.

> **"At this stage of my life, as I look back on everything that has happened to me, I am most proud of the fact that I created entertainment and an escape for people. This escape allows people to get out of their day-to-day situation and think about the world at large.**
>
> **"Only when we rise above our current circumstance and escape from the day-to-day can we really explore the possibilities."**

In speaking about physical conditions (such as blindness) that can create temporary roadblocks on our journey to success, Mr. Fairbanks said,

> **"It is all very well for people who are not blind to preach and lecture in alternative blessings, but I doubt if it is in any way helpful or a consolation. Still, there are many blessings**

which are available to those with the will and imagination—and the guts—to seek them out, polish them, and then use them as they are intended to be used."

It might be tempting at times to use a physical challenge as an excuse for not succeeding, but it is smarter to go around, over, under, or through the obstacle so that you can take advantage of the good things waiting for you on the other side.

# DONNA FARGO

## "EVERYBODY HAS A SONG"

**M**any years ago, it seemed that you couldn't turn on your radio without hearing the song "The Happiest Girl in the Whole U.S.A." It was Donna Fargo's first record, and first big hit. Thanks to that song and its follow-up hit, "Funny Face," she won such awards as "Top Female Vocalist," "Single of the Year," "Song of the Year," and "Best Selling Female Country Artist."

What happened to the "Happiest Girl" after that first blush of success? She achieved international fame, saw her records go gold and platinum in several countries . . . and then found out that she had multiple sclerosis. But this is a woman who knows how to fight, and with her M.S. in remission, she continues to do the work she loves.

Donna Fargo sent me a five-page, single-spaced letter in response to my request for her comments on success. Her closing paragraph alone gives us a good idea of how this singer made it to the top, and why she can still be considered a success after all this time, so I'll share that with you first.

> **"I hope your project helps you achieve your own definition of success as you seek to help**

others apply the information and impressions in your book to their own lives. If I have helped you in any way by doing this, then I have helped myself and have contributed to my own success and happiness."

And now, here is more of what Donna Fargo had to say about success and happiness:

"I think true success is attained through the personal satisfaction of doing what one feels called to do in life.

"In my case, I always wanted to be a singer . . . I just responded to this dream and accepted it, just as I accepted the color of my eyes . . .

"My goal wasn't to make money, or to make records at first, particularly. I just wanted to sing. I would call it a burning desire. I don't think I chose this dream. I think, rather, it chose me . . .

"My feelings of success came when I began writing songs that I actually liked and later, singing them in front of audiences. Other manifestations of my success came when I began to receive awards. These awards made me feel accepted and recognized by my peers, . . . so they were exciting and fulfilling. But, if I hadn't felt the personal satisfaction that I was doing something that I loved that inspired my very being, that made me very proud, happy, useful, and that allowed me to give something to others and receive back from them, . . . I don't think I would have known the meaning of success. . . .

"Once a man brought his children with him to one of my concerts. He came backstage and introduced himself and said, 'Donna, I want you to know how much your song "Happiest Girl in the Whole U.S.A." has impacted our lives. These are my seven children. My wife just died. "Happiest Girl" was her favorite song. We played it at her funeral. The kids wanted to come and tell you this story, and how much your song meant to them and their mom.' I cried, but they were smiling. They said, 'Don't cry, Donna. We want you to be happy. She was happy. She loved *your song.*'

"A Grammy might symbolize success materially, but this story symbolized the real Grammy to me—a deeper meaning of success. The song reflected a reality in someone's life and gave them a melody and some words to sing along with, even for just a short time . . .

"I believe everybody has a song—not necessarily *literally* a song to be sung, but I mean here a song as a symbol of a calling in life. I believe we all have something special to do in life. We don't have to change the world, but I believe we are expected to use our uniqueness to make some difference, small though it may be . . .

"I really think happiness is very closely aligned with success, and may almost be an interchangeable synonym. Happiness (like success) also comes from doing what we feel called to do in life; however, it's also obvious no one can experience one without the other.

"I think it is easier to be happy when we feel balanced in all the areas of life we're involved in. I think happiness is symbolized most often by a state of rest. It is being able to face life knowing that your God is with you and won't forsake you.

"It is not always getting what you like but liking what you get."

In closing her letter to me, Donna Fargo added a statement that applies to each of us:

"Good luck on your journey. Get the 'map' out to follow the right roads toward your own destiny."

# $\mathcal{A}$RT $\mathcal{F}$ERRANTE

## "COVER ALL YOUR BASES"

The story of Art Ferrante, as you will see, is also very much the story of Lou Teicher. Ferrante and Teicher began their career as a piano duo in 1947 and proceeded to tour with leading orchestras and to record 30 albums.

Art Ferrante describes himself as a "frustrated writer." He sent me some wonderful samples of his work, and I chose the one that I feel best illustrates what it takes to become a success—not just in music, but in every field. (Hint: It has to do with determination.)

Mr. Ferrante calls this true story, "Sorry, Baby—Better You Than Me."

> "In the early 1950s, finding two concert grand pianos in the same city was something of an occupational hazard. The solution for us was to supply our own. We hocked ourselves to the bone, bought a truck, a dolly, two skid-boards and a couple of dozen blankets and belts, and away we went.

"Our first tour was booked by us. We created a fictional agent. Called him Chuck Ward (very American). Sent out 3,000 letters under his aegis to colleges and various concert organizations both in the United States and Canada. In return, we received eight inquiries. We accepted them all. It didn't matter where the cities were.

"In order to play those eight engagements, we had to cover 7,400 miles in a truck. We drove the truck, tuned the instruments, assisted in the moving, and offered our expertise in the assembling and disassembling of the pianos.

"The truck was a cab-over-engine type (not unlike a delivery van). It was possible to walk from the cab directly into the body of the truck. The pianos lay on their straight sides, each atop its own skid-board with pedals, lyres, and legs removed. They were blanketed and then fastened to cast-iron rails that ran along the inner sides of the van. We would take turns sleeping on the floor, between those huge pianos, while the other did the driving.

"In those days there were no interstates, and many of the two-lane highways were in pretty bad shape. Every time we hit a severe bump, the pianos would bounce, and the clang of the sound-board would awaken the fellow sleeping on the floor. He would open his eyes, check the belt buckles, take a sigh of relief, and go right back to sleep. Nine-foot concert grands are very big pianos, but when you're lying on your back between them, they are *enormous*.

"Three of those eight concerts were in Canada. Some nights, while we were on the move, it got so cold we'd swipe a couple of blankets from the pianos. Gently patting them on their curves, we'd say, 'Sorry, Baby—better you than me.'"

They say that artists have to suffer for their craft. I'd say that Ferrante and Teicher went above and beyond the call of duty. And so did their pianos.

# ROMAN GABRIEL

## "PUSH YOURSELF"

When I was growing up, my best friend down the street owned the prized possession of the neighborhood: an authentic Roman Gabriel football helmet. I know we're not supposed to covet things that belong to others, but that football helmet was a major stumbling block for me in that area!

Years later, my friend and I trained together, and both of us made the National Weightlifting Team. As we were packing to go on one of our competition tours, he discovered the Roman Gabriel helmet in his closet. He asked me if I wanted it, but as this was many years later, it did not hold the same magic. But I revisited the initial excitement I'd felt as a small boy when Roman Gabriel agreed to submit his thoughts for this book.

Roman Gabriel was an All-American at North Carolina State University. He began his professional career with the Los Angeles Rams in 1962, and broke just about all of the Rams' passing records. Six years later, he was named the NFL's Most Valuable

Player. In his heyday, he even appeared in a John Wayne movie, *The Undefeated.*

Of all the letters I received as I was preparing this book, only one came in the form of a poem. This is what Roman Gabriel has to say about success:

## THE WINNER

It's hard to be a winner!
You have to push yourself to run the race.
Everyone cares if you practice
With 110% as the pace.

If you feel kind of poorly at game time,
You tighten your lip and go.
There's no way out so don't worry,
Because your teammates will always know.

You always think about winning,
Concentration will take care of old number one.
Then when the going gets rugged,
You play harder until the final gun.

Living the role of the winner,
You are always a hero in life.
There's room for whining and complaining,
But you never yell loud enough to cause strife.

Preparing and hustling at full speed,
You stay away from being called a jerk.
Strive for more than you have to,
And there's no problem with the extra work.

Teamwork and Dedication,
This makes a winner of you.
Keep your head up and follow the rules,
Because you know they're not new.

You're only as good as your last performance.
Be responsible and accept some blame!
Don't let everyone else shoulder the load.
A winner knows that's not the name of the game.

If this is the game you want to play,
You really have nothing to fear.
You get to work every morning
And smile and organize your gear!

# PETER GRAVES

## "SUCCESS? MISSION: POSSIBLE"

It was my pleasure to meet and interview Peter Graves in 1996. No doubt he will always be best known for his work on the long-running television series *Mission: Impossible*. In more recent years, however, he has made his mark as host of the award-winning *Biography* program on the A&E network.

As much as anyone I have ever worked with, Peter Graves impresses me as a true professional. He goes to work and does his job to the best of his ability, whether he is doing a movie, a commercial, a *Biography* program, or an interview such as the one he did for NTN.

When I talked to him about success, this is how he summed it up:

> "I guess success in life means many different things to many different people, but it certainly was most important to me that I had a goal that I had my eye on.

"That goal was 'something I must do,' and I
persevered until I got it done or got a start at it."

After you reach the goal or start to make headway on it, I
wanted to know, what comes next?

"Then you stay on top of it, and keep punching
and pushing and striving all the time to go in
the directions that you want, [after] whatever it
is in life that you want."

Success, then, is not a matter of "arriving," but of scaling one
mountain and using it as a jumping-off point for the next peak.

If you want to be successful, this is a mission you must accept.

# Alexander Haig

## "Do Your Level Best"

In the U.S., you don't get much more successful than being named Secretary of State. And you don't get chosen for that post unless you have outstanding credentials and experience.

Alexander Haig more than met the requirements of the job. He is, after all, a graduate of the U.S. Military Academy, the Naval War College, and the Army War College. He became a general in 1973, was chief of staff at the White House, and served as commander-in-chief of the U.S. European command. He is definitely someone you want to talk to when you are writing a book on success.

In responding to my request for his comments, this is what he wrote:

> "Whatever you do, make a difference.

> "Practice rather than preach. Make of your life an affirmation, defined by your ideals, not the negation of others. Dare to the level

of your capability, then go beyond to a higher level. If you would be fit to command men, obey God."

I might add . . . if you can't be a leader, be the best follower you can possibly be. When you do your best, you are a success.

# MONTY HALL

## "GET A GOOD NIGHT'S SLEEP"

On a television game show, who really wins? Is it the contestant who receives the new car, the $25,000, and the vacation of a lifetime? Is it the members of the audience who share in the excitement of the moment? Is it the members of the crew for whom the show provides steady employment? Or perhaps it's the show's creator, who earns a small fortune from syndication rights.

Yes, all those people derive some degree of happiness from a game show. But in the case of Monty Hall, host of the long-running (22 years!) *Let's Make A Deal*, it was the emcee who walked away a winner.

In the midst of, and especially after a successful show like *Deal*, you could understand it if the star decided to simply do his job and be a good citizen. But Monty Hall wouldn't rest until he shared his bounty with others. Are you looking for happiness? Read this and learn.

"When I was a youngster, I never thought I would grow out of the poverty of my surroundings. Fate was kind to me, and I managed to achieve more than I ever dreamed of. Thus, I can honestly say I never was hungry for even greater success.

"My television success brought me fame and financial rewards. But it is the way I used these, that is the real secret of my happiness. I have a great marriage, wonderful children and grandchildren, and have devoted my life to helping others. I spend 200 days a year traveling, speaking, and raising money for countless charities.

"There is a saying, 'It is better to give than to receive.' I place my own creed next to that. 'There are givers and takers in the world. The takers eat well; the givers sleep well.'

"I sleep well."

# HELEN HAYES

## "SET THE STAGE"

I was privileged to interview the first lady of the American stage, Helen Hayes, late in her life. I see her as an actress who bridged the worlds of movies and theatre better than anyone before or since.

During each of my celebrity interviews, I ask movie stars about other people they have worked with. Not all of the comments are positive. But I have never heard anyone say anything but the very best about Helen Hayes.

I asked her what she wanted to be remembered for.

> "I will be remembered however I am remembered. I have no control over that.
>
> "The things I value are the efforts I have made on behalf of my craft and the theatre, in general, that no one will ever know about.
>
> "I have attempted to be a great force for the stage and theatre as a whole."

It was important for Helen Hayes and it is important for us to see our work as something that will result in something larger than our own individual contribution. To realize a meaningful success, we need to work for "the greater good," and not for a flowery eulogy.

# KATHARINE HEPBURN

## "PURSUE YOUR PASSION"

Narrating movies and TV shows to make them accessible for blind and visually impaired people was all we had in mind when we created the Narrative Television Network. There was no thought of my doing celebrity interviews for a talk show.

In 1989, we got a huge break and were able to launch our network with several hundred affiliates across the country. As part of the deal, I agreed to deliver two-hour blocks of programming at various times of the day and night throughout the week. The problem was, our movies did not fit that time schedule, so we were faced with dead air time on national television. To fill this dead time, my immediate thought was to conduct interviews with the movie stars who appeared in the movies we were showing.

And so, we went to the library and found a book entitled *Addresses of the Stars*. We mailed letters to some of the biggest names in show business, asking them to be a part of this new network. The first positive response I received was from Katharine Hepburn. I knew this was big, but I didn't know *how* big. You see, every celebrity who called to inquire about the show would ask what other guests had already been on. Being able to tell them that Katharine Hepburn had been on the show opened every door.

Between 1933 and 1981, Miss Hepburn won four Oscars and received eight additional Academy Award nominations for her work. *The Philadelphia Story, Guess Who's Coming to Dinner,* and *The African Queen* are three of her most memorable films. Someone as celebrated as she should be used to the interview process, but Miss Hepburn is a very private person to whom interviews do not come easily. For this reason, I will always be grateful to her for sitting down and talking with me.

I remember asking her about her career and what she might have done had she not been an actress.

**"I am thankful that I can make a living as an actress. If I could not, I would have to find another way to support myself as I pursue my passion."**

Katharine Hepburn taught me, then, that nothing succeeds bigger or better than a driving passion for your life's work. All of us need to find that passion in our work, or find work where we can experience the passion.

Most jobs don't come with annual awards ceremonies, but we can feel like winners as long as we do what we absolutely love.

# CHARLTON HESTON

## "SPEND TIME WISELY"

**W**hen we first started the Narrative Television Network and the very special work we do, we were struggling for credibility in the broadcast, cable, and entertainment industries. There were several people who took the time and effort to write us a letter of support and encouragement. One of the first letters we received was from Charlton Heston. It meant everything to us then, and it still does today. That letter is displayed in our office.

Charlton Heston has played roles such as Moses and Ben Hur that will forever make him seem larger than life. The reality is, he has a life larger than that of the ordinary person. But his message to us is that we *all* can live larger than life.

One of the most powerful lessons that Charlton Heston can teach us is not about stardom or career, but about personal and family life:

> "The best thing my wife, Lydia, and I gave our
> children was our time, which we did not so

much out of a feeling that we must ('quality time'. . . what an ugly phrase), but because we liked it.

"Love is, or should be, a given.

"I *liked* driving (my daughter) Holly to ballet lessons, or lip-syncing show tunes with her to records while she cavorted in makeshift costumes, just as Lydia liked teaching both kids to swim, and we both loved reading to them."

In his autobiography, *In the Arena*, Charlton Heston said that in looking back, there was nothing he would want to change, that life had been "too good" to him. Perhaps that is because with all his success in the world of entertainment, the world he created with his family managed to stay center stage.

# LOU HOLTZ

## "GO WITH WHAT YOU KNOW"

F ootball coach Lou Holtz led Notre Dame to the national championship in 1988 in just his third year on the job. In 1988-89, his team also achieved its longest consecutive winning streak—23 games.

The job of head football coach at Notre Dame is considered by many to be the best coaching job in the nation. It was a job that Lou Holtz had earned. He began his coaching career in the late 1950s while he was working on his bachelor's degree, and went on to coach at several other colleges and universities, and at one point, with the New York Jets.

When he was named National Coach of the Year in 1988, Lou Holtz appeared to have reached the pinnacle of success. When he lost his job nearly a decade later, it looked like the end of a dream. As it happened, I had written to ask him for his comments on success at precisely the time his tenure at Notre Dame was coming to an end. What he had to say—to me, and to all who wrote to him at that difficult time—was:

". . . I feel blessed to have had the opportunity to coach at the University of Notre Dame.

"I do not know what the future holds, but I do know who holds the future."

You get the impression that no matter where Lou Holtz finds himself, his outlook on life is going to see him through every time.

# Lamar Hunt

## "Work Together"

Many people dream of someday owning a professional sports franchise. For Lamar Hunt, that dream became a reality when he founded the National Football League's Kansas City Chiefs in 1959.

In a sport like football, the goal is always success, but failure is more often the reality. Injuries, coaching changes, contract disputes, and trades can turn a winning team into a losing one. It's easy to keep up player morale when things are going well, but what do you do when nothing is working? How do you grab success from the jaws of failure? Lamar Hunt wrote to me:

> "I have found that whether in the field of sports or in everyday life, one must possess many of the same qualities in order to achieve success. Some of these qualities would include dedication, hard work, honesty, integrity, leadership, loyalty, self-discipline, treating people fairly, teamwork, and having a positive

attitude. Equally important to this foundation is a strong sense of duty to family and friends, and service to society.

"As a leader, it is imperative that you be able to convey your vision to other people. . . . You should try to focus on the wants and needs of others and help them achieve their personal goals. This will not only show your concern for them, but will ensure their dedication to achieving your goals as well."

In other words, do unto others as you would have others do unto you. I think I remember reading that somewhere.

# MARTY INGELS

## "DON'T BE AFRAID"

M arty Ingels started out in 1957 as a comedian and an actor. By 1964, he had "made it." He was the star of his own television sitcom, he was young and healthy, and the future looked very bright indeed. But within a year, his show was canceled, and it seemed possible that he might lose not just his career, but his life.

When Marty Ingels wrote to me, he said that his story wouldn't be like any of the others in this book, and he was right. Believe it or not, he says that the biggest stumbling block on his road to success was *success itself.*

> "When you think about it, aren't there many people you know who are as *afraid* and *intimidated* by the very 'achievement' they claim to seek, as they are driven and dedicated to it?
>
> "For me, it was a constant ambivalent agony. In my head there were two loud and unceasing voices, one pushing me on every minute of every

day to uncompromising victory everywhere,
assuring me always of my capability and my
worth; and the other, mocking, deriding, and
sabotaging all of it at every turn, undermining
and decrying each step forward with a thousand
frightful reasons to fall back and lose."

Ingels thought he had this problem under control, but
everything came crashing down one night on—of all places—
*The Tonight Show*. There he sat with Johnny Carson, his every
move being observed by millions of people—and he lost it. As he
was telling one of his usual funny stories, he noticed a
"trembling" in his toes and his right leg. He didn't know it at that
moment, but it was the beginning of an earthquake that would
change his life.

"I had had anxiety attacks before," he said, "but
this one was different. It was unyielding and
horrendous and it wasn't going away. By now my
whole body was numb, and tingling like a zillion
little needles. It was like I was just 'slipping away,'
little by little, right there on network television.
And the more I fought it, the more I twisted and
turned in that chair, trying to sit on my hands and
rattle my feet, the louder the audience laughed.
Crazy Marty was at it again. What a card!"

To get himself offstage, he stood and announced that he would be the first guest to ever use Johnny Carson's private bathroom. The audience was still laughing when he staggered away. Some members of the backstage crew drove him home, wrapped him in a blanket, and left him on the floor in front of his television set.

*Whatever this mindboggling seizure is,* Marty told himself, *it'll be gone in the morning.* But this time he was wrong.

For the next nine months, three weeks, and four days, Marty Ingels lay on that very spot in that dingy apartment building. Had it not been for a neighbor, he said, who brought him hot food, he would have died.

To this day, no one knows exactly what brought him down.

**"Whatever it was that KO'd me for all those long and agonizing months, found it timely to just disappear . . . all at once . . . one Sunday afternoon, just like that, and bring me back to life again . . . older, wiser, stronger for what I'd survived, and determined to keep the list of fervent promises I had made to myself while I was down there, bent and beaten. [Those promises] spoke of not making any of the mistakes I'd made before, of having the strength to hold tight to the dream, no matter what, and most of all, of never being scared again—for**

**what, now, was there to be scared *of*? I had
already been beyond the gates of hell, and there
were no other places left but UP."**

He knew he wanted to stay in the business, so he started a
company called Celebrity Brokerage. It's the largest and most
successful packager of celebrity endorsements in the world.

I believe Marty Ingels is right. Many people say they want to
succeed, but, in truth, the thought of doing so absolutely terrifies
them. They find ways of sabotaging themselves so that their
greatest fear—actually making good—won't be realized. Others
achieve success and feel undeserving of it, or unable to maintain
it over the long haul, so they, too, sabotage themselves and
thereby relieve themselves of the burden of being on top.

Success is not a bad thing! It requires hard work and
sacrifice, but it's a worthwhile pursuit. As long as you're going
after it for the right reasons, and as long as it will produce healthy
benefits in your life and the lives of those you love, it's nothing
to be afraid of.

# LYNN JOHNSTON

## "RECOGNIZE YOUR GIFTS"

Back in 1979, a new comic strip made its debut, and it has been delighting readers ever since. Called *For Better or For Worse*, it presents the adventures and misadventures of the Patterson family: Elly, John, Michael, Lizzie, and April. The strip's creator, Lynn Johnston, has watched her brainchild find its way into newspapers all over Canada, the U.S., and in 21 other countries, and has picked up a Pulitzer Prize nomination along the way.

When I got in touch with Lynn Johnston and told her a little about the Narrative Television Network, she remembered an experience from several years ago that I think has a lot to say about the kinds of limits we place on ourselves and the need to search out new possibilities if we want to be successful.

> "When I was 19," she said, "a friend of mine carved a mountain out of jade. It was a piece about eight inches long and six inches high. When I asked him why he had carved a mountain, he told me he wanted it to 'show' a

friend who was blind, what a mountain was by letting him feel the angles and the peaks and the natural shapes in stone.

"I have always known that I was particularly blessed with the gift of sight. I have also known that I could easily lose this gift, and have considered, often, what I would do if I were to have to rely on all of my other senses and gifts to continue to do the things I love to do, which are: to create, to storytell, to laugh and make others laugh, to play an instrument (but learn to play it well). I know I would survive, but it would be an overwhelming challenge.

"I know that I would change, that my more dormant gifts would emerge—and I realize, perhaps, that being sighted can actually limit one's talents in a way by focusing an artistic bent towards the visual forms of expression."

Lynn Johnston, a successful cartoonist, also had these words of encouragement for anyone who thinks he was standing in the wrong line when strengths and abilities were being handed out:

"The talents we have are immeasurable. The resources and the possibilities for success are as far away as your willingness to pursue and work hard for them.

"I have always admired people who have developed their lives and their skills far surpassing the difficulty that might be perceived as a handicap. Not because they have done so in *spite* of their difference, but with the aid of it. They teach me, once again, that anything *I* want to do I can do, and I *will* no matter what."

All of us have mountains in our lives. Lynn Johnston has shown us that they can be things of beauty, objects of instruction . . . and a lot of fun to climb.

# $\mathcal{S}$HIRLEY $\mathcal{J}$ONES

## "WRITE YOUR OWN RULES"

When we talk about success, we sometimes forget that it isn't just about our careers. It's also about our families. So, I'm glad that when Shirley Jones answered my request for her thoughts on success, she chose to send me something she wrote that has to do with making a success of marriage.

She could have talked about landing the lead role of Laurey in her first movie, the musical *Oklahoma!*, or winning the Academy Award for *Elmer Gantry*, or being one of America's favorite moms on the television series *The Partridge Family*. Instead, she sent me the script of an anniversary card she created for her husband, Marty Ingels, on their tenth anniversary. Called "The Ten-Word Manual for Marriage," it has some tips that also apply to getting along with people you *aren't* married to. (Let's face it: If you know how to get along with people, you are a lot more likely to succeed in *all* the areas of your life.)

I want to share just a few of Shirley Jones's "Ten Words" with you.

"TRUTH. The only way to go, with anything, especially love. And there is absolutely no defense against it; it is the purest communication there is. Try it, with yourself first. . . . Work on it. It will lift all the weight off your shoulders.

"HUMOR. Easier said than done, but do it, find it, feel it, look for partners with it. Life's absurd as it is. Try laughing at it. Just make the *sound* first. It's contagious, and medicinal, and addictive.

"SELF-ESTEEM. The magic words. If you won't muster any for you, nobody else will. . . . Any spare time, work on liking yourself better. It'll put a new paint job on everything.

"CHANGE. There's always someone to tell you you have to. *Wrong. Don't.* Rather, spend time finding out who you *really are.* Work on being more of *that.* A lot better than the futile 'gotta change' treadmill, which never really ends."

There are lots of books (with lots of lists) that presume to tell you how to live your life. My advice: Pull out only the concepts that you believe will work for *you*, and then make your *own* list.

As Shirley Jones has shown us, we can look at who and where we are, decide what and where we want to be, and come up with *our own plan* for getting the most out of our lives. It won't be easy, but it will definitely be worth the effort.

Her advice must have worked, as her handwritten note at the end of her letter stated, "They didn't give our marriage three months. Next November, we celebrate our twentieth year. We must be doing *something* right!"

# DEBORAH KERR

## "ONE THING CAN LEAD TO ANOTHER"

D eborah Kerr was in one of those unique movies in a very special role that people will never forget. Appearing opposite Burt Lancaster in *From Here to Eternity*, hers was a portrayal that captivated audiences. And yet, being an actress was not her dream.

As we were talking about her career, she taught me a lesson from her life that can benefit all of us. It concerns being honest with ourselves about what we can and cannot do.

"From as early as I can remember, I wanted nothing in the world as much as to be a ballet dancer.

"I remember my mother taking me to the ballet, and I was simply enchanted with the ballerinas. After studying ballet for several years, I realized that I was much too tall to ever be a great ballet dancer. However, pursuing dance gave me an appreciation for performing which carried me into a great and fulfilling career as an actress."

There are some limitations that simply cannot be overcome. But instead of giving up on *all* your dreams just because your first dream can't come true, transfer your enthusiasm to a new endeavor.

Deborah Kerr became a great actress who was nominated six times for an Academy Award. She never won. But she *did* win the New York Critics Award and the Sarah Siddons Award.

And in 1994, she finally received that elusive Academy Award: an honorary Oscar for career achievement.

# THE AMAZING KRESKIN

## "STOP AND LISTEN"

The Amazing Kreskin has appeared in countless performances around the world for more than 50 years. As a mentalist, he is one who perceives and reads other people's thoughts. Although most would consider this a gift, Kreskin believes it is an ability that, to a certain degree, can be developed.

In his letter to me, he said that oftentimes, when a person loses his eyesight late in life, his hearing becomes more acute. He hears someone approaching from a distance, long before the sighted person who is with him is aware of it. And in some cases, he knows *who* is approaching before he receives any aural cues.

What does this have to do with success? It tells us that if we have a weakness in one area, we can develop a strength in another in order to compensate. It also tells us that *we need to listen* if we are going to get the information we need to come to a correct conclusion . . . or come up with a sensible solution.

"Orson Welles once said to me, 'The worst thing that happened to movies was color,'" Kreskin said. "It was too distracting. Motion and action that attracts the eye can often detract from our inner sensitivity to what is being said or done before us." In other words, we put so much emphasis on what we see that we get lazy in our efforts to listen to, and interpret the meaning of, what is being said.

Kreskin said he looks upon his work as an adventure, and himself as "an adventurer exploring probably the greatest riddle of all: the human mind." He gave this advice:

> **"To those who do not exhibit my abilities as a thought reader, I might give my strongest advice, and that is to listen and listen fully before responding or commenting on something that is said or mentioned in a conversation. Pause and listen.**
>
> **"Too many people are afraid of silence. It is as if something has to be happening all the time. But often, with silence, there is more happening. There is a reflection on what was really said to us, what was really meant by the remarks, and, yes, perhaps some passage of thought between that person and ourselves."**

You don't have to have ESP to get ahead, but you do need to PAY ATTENTION.

# DOROTHY LAMOUR

## "HAVE A SENSE OF HUMOR"

**D**orothy Lamour will always be remembered for her roles in the *Road* shows, a series of movies she did with Bob Hope and Bing Crosby. She also had the good fortune of being considered one of the most beautiful women of her time. (Put a "G" in front of her last name, and you'll get the picture.)

When I interviewed her, she had a great perspective on the way that Hollywood sometimes works. She realized that her looks got her into the movies, but that her talent kept her working. And she was very pleased that beyond her devastating beauty, she simply brought people joy. She said to me:

> "As I look back, I am most proud that I made people laugh.

> "The world takes itself far too seriously; laughter is something there's far too little of. Whatever one does, they should always remember to laugh."

Dorothy Lamour was right. Not everything that happens to us —and certainly not every decision we make—is a matter of life and death. We need to lighten up a little, look on the bright side a little more often, and remember that it takes more muscles to frown than it does to smile.

If we can bring laughter into someone else's life, we will have achieved a very special kind of success.

# JANET LEIGH

## "MAKE THE WORLD BETTER"

S ay, "Janet Leigh," and what comes to mind is likely her chilling shower scene in *Psycho*. But her fans also loved her in the musical comedy *Bye Bye Birdie*, as well as in dozens of other films.

When I asked her to tell me what success and happiness mean to her, she shared with me a wonderful story about someone very near and dear to her. I think you will find it inspiring.

"My grandmother was blind, and it—it being the word and the condition—didn't mean much to me as a child. That was just the way she was, and she didn't seem so different from the rest of the family. She cooked, she ironed, she did the laundry, she chopped kindling, she played the piano.

"And then one day, after I found out what blind meant, I made believe I couldn't see. I shut my eyes tightly and attempted to do what I normally did. But I couldn't do anything. I became frantic and quickly opened my eyes so I could be safe again.

"But Grandma couldn't see even when she opened her eyes; she wasn't playing a game. It was at that time I realized what a great woman she was, and how courageously she had met and overcome a tremendous challenge. I never heard her complain, or say, 'Why me?' She was almost always smiling, caring, interested, and interesting.

"She taught me the greatest lesson in living that I could ever learn. Anytime I would feel blue, or unlucky, or deprived, or jealous, or anything negative—I would think of her, and understand how blessed I was.

"She made the world better because she was in it.

"My grandmother made me want to leave the world a better place than when I came into it— just like she had."

That's a worthwhile goal for all of us to have.

# JACK LEMMON

## "ROLL WITH THE PUNCHES"

One of my earlier interviews on NTN was with Jack Lemmon. Since that time, I have written plays and actually performed in a brief play in a show we produce called *Discover Your Destiny*. *Discover Your Destiny* is designed to create a complete theatre experience by taking my platform-speaking information and putting it together with celebrities on the big screen, music, lights, and drama.

I probably owe my exploration of playwriting and acting to Jack Lemmon more than to anyone else. He brings an energy and a passion to every role that few actors have ever managed to duplicate.

This Oscar-winning, Emmy-winning Harvard graduate is one of those rare actors who can do comedy as effortlessly as he does drama. He first appeared on Broadway at the age of 28. Soon after, he made his way onto television and then began the film career that has made him a fixture on the big screen for more than 40 years.

Many of Jack Lemmon's films have had to do with the issues of the day. *The China Syndrome* concerned the potential dangers of nuclear power plants. As you read what he had to say to me on the subject of success, I think you will agree that this enduring entertainer is a man who takes very seriously the impact he has on his audience.

> **"When I think about the accomplishments of my career, I do not look at the individual highs and lows but at the overall body of work.**
>
> **"We don't live and die on one success or failure.**
>
> **"I am pleased that my career has brought laughter and entertainment to people, but I consider it a rare privilege that I have caused people from time to time to stop and think about who they are and how they stand on important issues in their lives and in the world."**

Achieving success can be thrilling, but it is a lot more satisfying if you can make a worthwhile difference in someone's life on your way up.

# Art Linkletter

## "Watch Where You're Going"

At a very young age, I was diagnosed with a disease that would result in my blindness. Shortly after the diagnosis, I was invited to a positive thinking rally which featured some of the greatest speakers of all time. Art Linkletter was among them. He is a marvelous platform speaker, and has been a tremendous force in the entertainment industry.

If you were around in the late 1950s and early 1960s, you probably remember watching *Art Linkletter's House Party* on television. Who could forget his interviews with children, during which he would ask them simple, innocent questions—and often receive answers that brought to mind the phrase, "out of the mouths of babes"? Mr. Linkletter, of course, turned that phrase into "Kids say the darndest things," and even wrote a book by the same title.

He wrote several other books as well, including *How to Be a Super Salesman*, *Yes, You Can!*, *Public Speaking for Private People*, and *Linkletter on Dynamic Selling*. But when I asked him to send me his comments for this book, his reply had nothing to do with selling yourself or some product. It had to do with giving of yourself. I think you will enjoy this story.

> "For a good many years I visited and spoke at the Braille Institute here in Los Angeles during their Christmas celebrations, and I know how much more joyful they make the holiday season. Occasionally something happens to underscore the rewards that I have received from being a part of their programs.

> "About two years ago following one of these appearances, I was out having a Sunday joy ride with my family in Beverly Hills and inadvertently made a left-hand turn at an intersection without noticing that a man was on the curb with a white cane and a Seeing Eye dog.

> "He stepped off the curb, and even though I was proceeding slowly and slammed on my brakes immediately, he walked into the fender and fell down. Naturally, I was horrified at having caused a blind man to fall down, and was relieved when he appeared to be all right. But right after, the thought of potential

headlines occurred to me, since in these litigious days, any well-known person can be hauled through courts and the tabloids as a result of even a minor accident such as this one.

"In assisting him to his feet and blurting out my profuse apologies, he stopped me by saying, 'Aren't you Art Linkletter? I think I recognize your voice because two days ago you were entertaining us at the Braille Institute.' I acknowledged that I was the same and apologized again, and he stopped me and said, 'Don't worry, please, about this accident; you will have no problems with me. And even if you had run over me, what you do for us at Christmastime is worth so much that I would forgive almost anything you could do.'

"Talk about bread cast upon the waters!"

He's right. You never know when one of your acts of kindness will come back to you in a timely, beneficial way.

There is another quote attributed to Mr. Linkletter that ties in with the idea of putting something in to get something out. Of course, we should never "give to get," but there are times when we need to give our best effort in order to achieve the success we are after.

"People find gold in fields, veins, river beds, and pockets. But wherever you find gold, it takes work to get it out."

Let's roll up our sleeves and get to work.

# Bob Losure

## "Self-Pity Is Self-Defeating"

When I was growing up in Tulsa, Oklahoma, there was one traffic reporter in town. His station didn't have a helicopter, so whenever he reported a traffic jam, he was usually stuck in it. Yes, I will always remember Bob Losure as KRMG Radio's *Man On the Move.*

Bob Losure lived up to his title. He moved from radio to television in 1976, becoming a popular Tulsa anchorman and reporter. He moved again several years later when he was offered the chance to be an anchor on CNN *Headline News* in Atlanta. It sounds as if all these moves were normal transitions in the life of a journalist, but I think you should know the real story. I believe it will be an inspiration to you. Here's what Bob Losure had to say:

> "Life is not going to be easy. For every 'up,' there seems to be a 'down,' and so much of what we make of this brief time on earth depends on how we view life. I was sailing

along, expecting to live to at least 75 or 80, when I discovered that wasn't necessarily so in 1985. I had *cancer.*"

Two difficult operations later, Bob Losure found himself lying in a hospital bed, a tube "up my nose and down my throat into my stomach to prevent me from aspirating and dying in my own fluids." He was told that some of the lymph nodes that had been removed from his chest were cancerous, "but I went back to work, thinking I needed my job . . . more than I needed to take the chemotherapy treatments that would almost certainly prevent [the cancer's] return."

Two months later, the cancer came back. Chemotherapy saved his life. Three months later, he was out of the hospital—cured. He has been cancer-free for more than a decade.

He said:

"I needed to look for a job and, ironically, it forced me to set my sights higher. Through perseverance, I found a great one—at *CNN Headline News,* anchoring weekends and weeknights. Out of a tough personal dilemma, one door closed and another one opened because I refused to give up and feel sorry for myself.

"I don't let a day go by without thanking God. If I die tomorrow, I have had a full life. People have been wonderful to me, in the good times and the bad, and I've come to believe that you do indeed *reap what you sow.* For those who constantly gripe about life, I turn and walk away. For those who speak negatively about people behind their backs, I move on. For those who earlier believed I couldn't have a career as a television news anchor, I don't hear from them anymore.

"You are in charge of your life. Don't be afraid to change your focus if you're going down a road that you don't want to travel anymore.

"Advice from others is fine, but listen to what your intuition and your heart tell you is right.

"The cup, to me, is never half empty; it's half full.

"If you want to be remembered tomorrow as a kind, giving person who looks at strangers as *only friends they haven't met,* then today is the first *wonderful* day of the rest of your life."

# $\mathcal{T}$INA $\mathcal{L}$OUISE

## "REACH OUT"

There were lots of things on *Gilligan's Island* that puzzled us. The first question that most of us had, after watching the show a few times, was, "If it was only supposed to be a three-hour tour, why did they all take so much luggage?" Equally amazing was how Ginger Grant, the movie actress played to perfection by Tina Louise, managed to look glamorous on what had to be a hot and humid desert island—without the aid of a hair stylist or makeup artist!

Several years after *Gilligan's Island* ended its original run, Tina Louise popped up again in the first few episodes of *Dallas*. Since then, she has been doing something with her life that will ultimately have a greater impact than any of her screen work. I'd like to share with you the letter she wrote to me.

> "I would say happiness is contribution—contribution in some way that makes you feel good . . . a way of sharing yourself with someone else where you enlighten in some way.

> "For me, being a volunteer teacher in the public school system has been a great source of joy. Working with children and helping them to read is very exciting. I would say besides feeding the hungry, helping someone to read is very gratifying and important, both to the giver and the receiver."

Going from acting to volunteer teaching might seem like a drastic career change, but it's obvious that Tina Louise has made a smooth transition. Perhaps it has something to do with the philosophy she expresses here—a philosophy that puts any bad feelings she might have (about being out of the public eye) in their place.

> "If you have a negative thought, don't waste hours thinking about it. Simply direct yourself to something positive and keep repeating the positive until you eliminate the negative."

Some negatives can't be erased by just thinking them away, but changing our attitude about the negative things in our lives puts us in a better position to change what we can. And when we're willing to change, we usually find better ways to use our time.

# GISELE MACKENZIE

## "GIVE IT YOUR ALL"

G isele MacKenzie, a native of Canada, began her show business career on the radio. Soon she was making records, including a series of albums for children. In the U.S., she had her own television show in the late 1950s, and appeared on *The Sid Caesar Show* in the early 1960s. She followed up her TV work by touring the U.S., singing the lead in musical comedies such as *The King and I.*

Here is her take on success and happiness:

> "Try to find the kind of job that you truly enjoy— in other words, if you don't like your job, switch to something that you will enjoy. Because then you will be contributing to the world-good and to your happiness. *Only* then will you be truly successful.
>
> "Success means accomplishment—in any field or job.
>
> "Whatever you do, do it well, with all your energy and heart."

# TIM McCARVER

## "MOVE OUT OF YOUR COMFORT ZONE"

I remember my summers when I was in elementary school. These were spent, in large part, listening to St. Louis Cardinal baseball on my transistor radio. I remember following every game on the radio and cheering for players I had never seen. One of my favorite players on the St. Louis Cardinals of my youth was Tim McCarver.

Being the catcher on a baseball team has to be one of the toughest jobs in sports. Even with all the protective armor, a catcher is the one who gets "taken out" when a player slides into home, and you know that has to hurt! Anyone who can endure that kind of abuse, year in and year out, must really be hooked on the game.

I think that describes Tim McCarver fairly accurately. He started out with the St. Louis Cardinals in 1959, and also played for the Philadelphia Phillies, the Montreal Expos, and the Boston Red Sox before retiring from the game in 1980.

Did I say retire? Tim McCarver didn't leave baseball. He became a sportscaster for the Phillies, the Mets, and ABC Sports before settling in with CBS Sports in 1990. In talking to me about success, he referred to his move from the Phillies to the Mets, and shared one of the secrets of making it to the top.

> "In my professional life, the most naked I have felt was when I moved from the Philadelphia Phillies to the New York Mets in 1983. I was very comfortable in Philadelphia, but had always heard that New York is the place to be. While that is true, New York City can also be a very lonely place when you are away from your family and consumed in work. However, I traded the security of a life with nominal practical rewards for a life fraught with speculation and the roll of the dice.
>
> "My confidence and professional staying power were certainly tested, but in looking back, it was worth the risk.
>
> "In the sportscasting field, New York is the place to be; three of the four networks are based there. If you can cut it, the chance for opportunity is there."

Once you have arrived at a place in your life that is satisfying and safe, it is tempting to stay right there. But if your dream is a little bigger than the opportunities being offered, sometimes you have to get out of the boat and swim for a distant shore.

# $\mathcal{L}$EE $\mathcal{M}$ERIWETHER

## "BRING COLOR TO SOMEONE'S WORLD"

To say the least, Lee Meriwether has had an interesting career. After being crowned Miss America 1955, she tackled television, appearing on *Time Tunnel*, *The New Andy Griffith Show*, *Barnaby Jones*, and *The Munsters*. In more recent years, she switched to daytime television, taking a role on *All My Children*.

I think there is an assumption that beauty queens have it made, that having a crown somehow makes them immune to the problems that mere mortals face. That hasn't been Lee Meriwether's experience. There was a time in her life when fame was worthless, and a child helped her turn things around.

This is what she said . . .

> "There he was, standing by my hospital room door, bracing his small body on a single crutch. A blue-eyed, tousled-blond-haired, midsized, handsome boy of ten or so with a soft southern accent and an easy, quick smile. He had heard

from the nurses down in pediatrics that I was in the hospital, with hepatitis. Whether he knew who I was, I'm not sure, but I was a sick puppy in a downward spiral of depression. I had been three days away from opening in a play there in New Orleans, and they had replaced me with Dina Merrill.

"He had a picture just for me that he had painted. It was a wonderful watercolor. Bright and happy, the scene was of his home. You could see it was filled with love. His family and a few animals were there, all going about their daily activities.

"His name was Christian Guillot, and he was hoping the picture would cheer me up. It did, but not just for the artistry or for the caring his good heart was sharing.

"It was in the picture itself that I realized the strength and courage of the young man before me.

"Through this act, he made me stop feeling sorry for myself. From that morning, I started to improve. Now, I'm not saying this was any miracle, but I did have a new attitude to face my situation, and the doctor commented that I was fighting now, and that was helping.

"I've kept in contact with Christian over the years. He's quite a celebrity in Louisiana.

"My memory of that day in the hospital, and of subsequent visits when we both received care at Ochners, returns often. I thank the good Lord for giving me the chance to have met this amazing young man. I've saved that picture he painted, and as always I draw strength from his little self-portrait down in the corner: a blue-eyed, tousled-blond-haired young boy with just one leg."

Each of us has the power to bring someone joy. Isn't it great that we don't have to be "perfect" to do so?

# RUSSELL MYERS

## "BORN TO DO IT"

When Russell Myers was working for Hallmark and trying desperately hard to break into the "funny papers," a friend of his suggested that he do a comic strip featuring a witch. He drew a character that he called *Broom-Hilda,* and that feisty little witch has been flying high ever since her first appearance in 1970.

When Russell Myers wrote to me to share his thoughts for this book, he let me in on a little secret: Comic strip characters have a mind of their own. Sometimes they write their own dialogue. Even if you create something, sometimes you have no control over what you have created. In Russell Myers's case, it seems to have worked out for the best.

I want to share his entire letter with you. I know you will enjoy it as much as you enjoy his work.

> "If I have learned anything, and there are those
> who will argue that hasn't happened yet, it is
> that in my work most of the fun in getting there
> is the getting there.

"There are many rewards to drawing a nationally syndicated comic strip. One nice one is that people send you money every month and you can eat food and have a house and shoes and sox. Another is that sometimes somebody says that they enjoy what you do. It's impossible not to smile when that happens.

"But I submit that most of us in this funny little business believe that we do what we do because we were born to do it. Each and every day we are doing what we are supposed to and it's fun. To sit in a room and write and draw little people that hop about on the page and say and do funny things, many of which surprise me as much as they do you, is a treat.

"I have trouble believing that any IRS agent or fish cleaner enjoys himself on the job. I have trouble believing that any cartoonist doesn't."

Imagine being paid to have fun. Russell Myers just proved that it is possible.

# $\mathcal{B}$ARRY $\mathcal{N}$EWMAN

## "WHEN YOU HAVE TO, YOU MUST!"

$\mathcal{B}$arry Newman's claim to fame was starring in the television series *Petrocelli*, for which he received an Emmy nomination and a Golden Globe Award.

For some actors, it would be enough to have one piece of work that makes them a household name. For Barry Newman, however, stardom was not the point. When he wrote to me in response to my request for his input, he sent back a brief paper entitled, "Barry Newman's Thoughts on How to Get the Most Out of Life."

**"The word for real success is 'passion'!**

**"You have to find something that you feel passionate about. If you have a dream that you cherish, a dream that you have to fulfill, whatever it may be, even if it sounds unrealistic to others, that is what you have to go after. Because that is what you are going to be successful in, because you put love and passion into it!**

"Most importantly, you should never go after a dream because of financial reasons. You may become rich, but end up dissatisfied and unhappy.

"I originally studied anthropology—an interesting subject. But just before I got my master's degree, I realized that I had to act.

"It is not important if you *want* to act, or *love* to act. But when you HAVE to act—you just HAVE to do it—then and only then, you must go for it and do it!

"And so I did. I did not have any money. I did not go *after* money. I struggled for years and years and studied and acted in every little play I could get my hands on. And because I made that choice for my life, in doing what I had the utmost passion for, I became successful, and happy.

"When I think back . . . if I had not achieved what I have achieved, I would still be happy that I had tried, and did what I loved.

"In short: Don't strive for money, wealth, power, and fame. It will come naturally, when you follow your passion."

# JUSTICE SANDRA DAY O'CONNOR

## "IT'S QUALITY THAT COUNTS"

S andra Day O'Connor was not well known outside judicial circles . . . until that day in 1981 when she became the first woman to be confirmed to the U.S. Supreme Court. A moderate conservative, she rose through the ranks, first as an assistant attorney general, majority leader of the Arizona Senate (the first U.S. woman to hold such a post), and a Superior Court judge.

In answering my request for her viewpoint on success, Justice O'Connor sent me a transcript of an address she delivered to a college graduating class. Some of the points she was driving home to these new graduates are points we would do well to take.

> "The person who really impacts on this world
> is, as has always been the case, not an
> institution, not a committee, and not a person
> who just happens to have a title; rather, it is the

truly qualitative individual. The qualitative individual *does* matter in this quantitative world of ours, now as ever."

Justice O'Connor went on to quote a passage from the Talmud that is also noteworthy:

"In every age, there comes a time when leadership suddenly comes forth to meet the needs of the hour. And so there is no man who does not find his time, and there is no hour that does not have its leader."

In explaining this passage, Justice O'Connor said:

". . . each of us, in our own individual lives and crises, will have a time to lead. Whether we will lead only a family, or a handful of friends, and when and how we will lead, is up to us, our views and our talents.

". . . the very nature of humanity and society, regardless of its size or complexity, will always turn on the act of the individual, and, therefore, on the quality of the individual."

You might scoff when you hear someone say, "One person can make a difference." But if a Supreme Court justice believes it can happen, I think we should start believing it, too.

# LUIS PALAU

## "CATCH FIRE!"

L uis Palau is an evangelist who has preached the gospel around the world. He grew up in Buenos Aires, Argentina, and decided to become an American citizen after completing his seminary studies in Oregon.

At one point during his seminary years, Luis Palau reached a crisis point. For a long time, he had believed that if he prayed enough, read enough, studied enough, and worked enough, he would succeed in his ministry. Despite these beliefs, he had a nagging feeling that somehow, he was missing the boat. He needed answers, but he couldn't find them anywhere.

Just before Christmas break, Major Ian Thomas, founder of a group that runs a Bible school in England, came to speak at the seminary. His brief talk opened Luis Palau's eyes to an important truth.

**"Major Thomas's theme was, 'Any old bush will do, as long as God is in the bush'" (speaking, of course, of the burning bush story in Exodus**

3:1–5). "The essence of his talk was that it took Moses forty years in the wilderness to realize that he was nothing. Major Thomas said God was trying to tell Moses, 'I don't need a pretty bush or an educated bush or an eloquent bush. Any old bush will do, as long as I am in the bush. If I am going to use you, I am going to use you. It will not be you doing something for Me, but Me doing something through you.'

"Major Thomas said the burning bush in the desert was likely a dry bunch of ugly little sticks that had hardly developed. . . . I realized I was that kind of bush: a worthless, useless bunch of dried-up old sticks."

His mistake, he said, was having too much pride in his accomplishments. That night he realized that

"everything in my ministry was worthless, unless God was in the bush. Only He could make something happen. Only He could make it work.

"I was thrilled to finally realize we have everything we need when we have Jesus Christ literally living in us.

"We cannot work for or earn our victories through any self-effort, any more than we can work for or earn our salvation."

When we have intelligence, talent, skills, a great personality, and the admiration of those around us, it's easy to start thinking that we are "self-made." We need to remember, as Luis Palau just said, that we don't do anything—or succeed in anything—alone.

# Gary Player

## "Put Problems in Their Place"

G ary Player has always stood for the very best things that golf embodies. He has the ability to be a total gentleman and a fierce competitor at the same time. I was very pleased when the Senior PGA Tour was developed. It gave a whole new generation an opportunity to learn about golf . . . and life . . . from Gary Player.

After entering the U.S. Professional Golfers' Association in 1955, he went on to win 31 tournaments, including the British Open, the Masters, the U.S. PGA, the U.S. Open, the South African Open (he was born in South Africa), the Australian Open, and the World Series of Golf. He was only the third player to win golf's Grand Slam.

By anyone's definition, this man is a winner. But as he told me, he has his ups and downs like everyone else. Listen to what he's learned . . .

**"Everyone has problems! It is part of our mortal experience. We have troubles to teach us**

patience, humility, and long-suffering, and most important, to bring us closer to our faith. However, it is not the problems that count but the manner in which we handle them. Our attitude is one of the most important fundamental aspects of our lives.

"We have the choice to make the best or the worst of any situation.

"Many years ago I was fortunate to read Norman Vincent Peale's book, *The Power of Positive Thinking,* and Dale Carnegie's book, *How to Win Friends and Influence People.* These excellent books helped me to achieve a good outlook, a positive approach, and [taught me] always to maintain a good sense of humour. 'Laugh and the world laughs with you, cry and you cry alone.'

"My great faith is most important in my life and in that of my family. This faith has given me courage to endure setbacks. Faith brings an inner peace and joy that is truly the peace of God that passes all understanding. . . . We need to keep God's Ten Commandments; they can always show us the way we must live. We need

to hold fast to the 'Iron Rod,' that being the
Word of God."

Mark Twain once said, "Golf is a good walk spoiled." I think
he would have seen the game in a whole new light if he'd had the
chance to tee off with Gary Player.

# JANE POWELL

## "FAMILY COMES FIRST"

**M**any of our NTN movies have featured Jane Powell, an actress who made a name for herself in the many musicals she did for MGM in the 1940s and 1950s. I have never interviewed her, but I have interviewed a number of people who worked with her. Probably the best description I heard, given by one of her co-stars, was the statement, "Jane Powell simply sparkles."

In the comments she sent to me concerning success, she wrote about balance. (I personally believe it is important to realize that balance does not mean limiting the things that you need to do for others. It means bringing total energy and "sparkle" to all the true priorities in our lives.)

Jane Powell said:

> "I am grateful for my career, but all my energies were never directed to just 'the career.' My family and home have always come first, and I do believe this balance has helped me keep my

sanity. (Don't put all your eggs in one basket, my mother used to say.)

"It is not easy to keep that balance and it takes constant awareness and effort, but with practice it gets easier.

"One must learn to say no! The freedom of that tiny word is one of the best lessons I have learned.

"Life is ever-changing—and so must we be willing to change—to fully appreciate and enjoy all of life's opportunities and adventures."

Jane Powell is a woman with very few regrets. We should all take a page out of her book.

# ORAL ROBERTS

## "FOLLOW YOUR CALLING"

I n *Who's Who*, Oral Roberts' profession is given simply as "clergyman," but he has done much more in his lifetime.

He pastored churches, conducted evangelistic crusades around the world, founded and served as president of the university that bears his name, taught, published magazines, appeared regularly on radio and television, and founded a retirement center and a medical and research center.

Controversy seems to follow Oral Roberts wherever he goes, but he knew from the beginning that the message he preached would never be a popular one to everyone who heard it. His parents, however, taught him early to "obey God." God Himself, he has said, spoke to him when he was a teenager. At the time, he was gravely ill with tuberculosis and was on his way to a tent meeting where an evangelist would pray for him. "Son," God said, "I am going to heal you and you are going to take My healing power to your generation." Oral Roberts was indeed healed, and did indeed do his best to fulfill the calling God has placed on his life.

Like so many successful men, Oral Roberts had a lot to overcome. His family was very poor. He was a stutterer who had to endure the taunts of his classmates. But he had dreams, and was determined to rise above his situation. For a time, he couldn't decide between preaching and becoming a lawyer. His parents' influence and his own faith—and the conviction that he had to obey God—helped him to make his choice. He never looked back.

"I'm an evangelist first and last," he said recently when I interviewed him for television. No one who has heard him preach can doubt that.

During some of his ministry's best years, he suffered some of his greatest personal tragedies. His older daughter and son-in-law died in a plane crash, and his older son committed suicide. What brought him through such terrible times of testing was, of course, his strong faith in God.

When it comes to the church, some say that success is measured by the size of the building, the number of members, the variety of programs offered, and the reputation of the pastor. For a man like Oral Roberts, however, whose work has gone so far beyond the traditional church structure, filling pews and earning the world's acclaim are not how God measures success. It all still comes down to obedience.

He went on to say in our interview:

"As I stand here today, I would do it all over again. I'd take every step. I'd make every journey. I'd fly every mile. I'd try to climb every mountain. I'd do it all over again. I wouldn't . . . change a thing. . . . I'd lay it upon me and upon you and upon everybody who will listen.

"I'd tell everybody to listen to God's voice."

If you don't do what you know in your heart that you are supposed to do, you will never find success.

# JIMMIE RODGERS

## "TRUST GOD"

A song called "Honeycomb," recorded in 1957, sent a singer named Jimmie Rodgers straight to the top of the charts. It turned out to be his one and only number-one hit, but he continued to record for another decade, making folk music in an age that gave center stage to rock and roll.

When I told Mr. Rodgers about this book, he wrote and said:

> "I really do not want to take credit for my own success. I was not a success until I put the whole process into God's hands. If there is anything I can add, it would have to be to trust Him and let Him show us the way. I gather strength from knowing that He will always be there for me, no matter what.
>
> "What God does not protect you from, He provides you through."

Jimmie Rodgers also had a story to tell about his father, the man who first told him how to become a winner in life.

"My father was a rough, tough little Irishman who loved to drink, and fight, and stir things up. Underneath was a man who loved his family with a passion. The neighborhood kids all called him 'Pop' because they, too, were part of his family. He cussed like a sailor, and would tell the preacher at the church that the sermon, that day, was the best 'blankety-blank' sermon he ever heard.

"Pop was hard on the outside and soft on the inside. He would put his head down and plow through everything that got in his way—and yet, he would stand under a tree and call a squirrel down to eat out of his hand.

"He lived long enough to see me become a national recording star, and he was very proud.

"Being a fighter, he only gave me one piece of advice. 'Jim,' he would say, 'keep your right hand high and your rear end off the floor.'

"God helps me do that every day. It's simple, but sometimes simple is best. Trust in God, and keep your right hand high and your rear end off the floor."

# $\mathcal{K}$ENNY $\mathcal{R}$OGERS

## "ICING ON THE CAKE"

Ihave had the opportunity of seeing Kenny Rogers several times in concert. Through all of his personal and professional challenges, he has never done a bad show. Whether you like his work or not, when you leave the concert hall, you know that you have just experienced the best that Kenny Rogers has to offer.

He began playing music in high school, dropped out of college to join a jazz trio, and was with the New Christy Minstrels before he formed the group that put him on the music map: Kenny Rogers and the First Edition. After a nine-year run with the group, he went solo, scoring a Grammy with a country song called "Lucille." The following year, he struck gold with a toe-tapping number called "The Gambler," a song that spawned several television movies.

Kenny Rogers looks like the kind of man who has been there, done that, and lived to tell about it . . . and he is. Just listen to what he has to say about success:

> "I consider success to be relative. When I was a
> kid, I lived in a federal housing project in
> Houston, Texas. To my knowledge, the most

money my father ever made was $75 a week. He was a wonderful man who lived during very tough times.

"I think that, as children, we all strive to improve on the accomplishments of our parents. I remember feeling successful the first week that I made more money than he did. While it was not much, it represented success to me.

"If young people can learn to set difficult, yet attainable goals, they establish themselves, in their own minds, as achievers.

"Success, however, does not guarantee you happiness. Interestingly enough, if you ask most people who are truly successful, I think that very few would say that their happiest moments were when they made their most money, but rather, when they felt the real possibility of achieving their dream.

"I was told, and I believe, that a person needs three things to be happy: someone to love, something to do, and something to look forward to.

"Happiness is just that simple. Success . . . simply the icing on the cake."

# CESAR ROMERO

## "NECESSITY CAN BE THE MOTHER OF JOY"

C esar Romero had a distinguished career in theatre and films. Like many actors, however, his crowning achievement came in the guise of a television role: as The Joker, on the *Batman* series.

Late in his life, he agreed to an interview. What we can learn from what he said is that sometimes, the dream finds *you*.

Thinking back over the years, Cesar Romero said:

> "Most of all, I am humbled and thankful for the career and the friends I have made. I started in this business simply as a way to support my family. But through the necessity of working, I found a true joy in my career.
>
> "As I look back, I realize it was the greatest thing that ever happened to me."

Sometimes you do what you have to do. And sometimes, if you're lucky, the thing you have to do becomes the thing you want to do more than any other. Open your heart and your mind to the possibilities.

# MAX SCHMELING

## "TODAY IS WHAT COUNTS"

B oxers get a lot of bad press. (Witness a fairly recent ear-biting incident.) That hasn't always been the case. In the 1920s and 1930s, a German boxer named Max Schmeling caught the imagination—and the admiration—of the world.

In his memoirs, Schmeling said, "It was a time that wanted heroes. As a boxer, I was a symbol."

He was also Germany's only world heavyweight boxing champion. As such, he was a man on whom many Germans pinned their hopes and dreams.

He won the title in 1930 against an opponent named Jack Sharkey. Two years later, Schmeling lost the rematch. But immortality was just around the corner. In 1936, he knocked out the previously unbeaten Joe Louis in what became known as the "Sensation of the Century."

In a 1938 rematch with Joe Louis, he was knocked out in the first round. Rather than bemoan his loss, however, he looked at the bright side and said, "A victory against Louis might have set me up as the Nazis' model Aryan."

Throughout his career, Max Schmeling was seen as an honest man without pretensions. Many wanted to use the boxer for their own purposes—including Hitler's Nazis—but he remained true to himself. When his career ended, he bought a farm, studied business, and obtained a production license from a major soft drink company.

It would be tempting, in his ninth decade (as he was in 1997), to sit around and dwell on what happened 60 years ago—to revisit the glory days, if only in his mind. But Max Schmeling has always been, if anything, a forward thinker.

He said when he was preparing to celebrate his 90th:

> **"I don't really think about the past. What matters is the present. And a huge interest in the future."**

They say that wisdom comes with age, but they don't say you can't cut a few corners and learn from someone else's experience. In a recent letter from Mr. Schmeling, he told me what a privilege it was to pass along his wisdom through this book. I think the lesson that Max Schmeling learned—live in the moment and look forward to tomorrow—is one we should all take advantage of *right now*.

# DR. ROBERT SCHULLER

## "SHARPEN YOUR FOCUS"

As founder and senior minister of the Crystal Cathedral in Garden Grove, California, Dr. Robert Schuller is one of the most visible ministers in America. His *Hour of Power* television program has been on the air for nearly three decades, and he has written more than two dozen books, with titles such as *You Can Become the Person You Want to Be* and *Tough Times Never Last, But Tough People Do.*

Dr. Schuller has been, for many years, an inspiration to me and to millions of people around the world. Most recently he has become a mentor and a friend. He was kind enough to endorse my first book, *You Don't Have To Be Blind To See,* and to submit some of his thoughts for *Success Secrets.* What he has to say about sight emphasizes, for me, the need to focus on what you're doing if you want to be successful.

**"Sight does not happen in the eye, even as hearing does not happen in the ear.**

"This is obvious. Sighted persons do not 'see' many things in front of them. They only 'see' what they are focused on, thinking about, aware of in their mind and spirit.

"So the person who is really blind is the person who is distracted from reality by anxieties or fears or other negative thoughts that . . . keep the center of his mental consciousness from really reading the thought that has come into [his] mind. . . . "

Until you learn to rely on your brain, rather than on what your eyes and your ears are telling you, you will never be able to "see" things as they truly are. And if you can't "see" exactly what is going on, you will find yourself making educated guesses about how to proceed. It's silly to stumble in the dark when the world's greatest computer—your brain—is at your disposal.

It's like they say: A mind is a terrible thing to waste. Use yours to fuel your drive to success.

# CHARLES SCHWAB

## "SEEK OUT NEW SOLUTIONS"

C harles Schwab is the chairman and chief executive officer of the brokerage house that bears his name. He is also the author of *How to Be Your Own Stockbroker.*

More importantly, he is chairman of the Parents' Educational Resource Center (PERC), a nonprofit agency that provides support and guidance for parents of children with learning differences, and the founding chairman of All Kinds of Minds, a nonprofit institute that promotes understanding and the best possible care of children with learning differences.

You see, Charles Schwab was diagnosed with dyslexia, a condition that makes reading and writing difficult. His son faces the challenge of dyslexia, too. Mr. Schwab founded PERC as a result of the experiences he and his wife had as they were trying to find help for their son.

When someone you love is challenged in some way, you want to do everything you can for him. I'm glad that people like

Charles Schwab don't stop there. I'm glad they take the time to look around and say, "Does anyone else have this problem? How can I help?"

Observe the way that Charles Schwab views what some would consider a negative condition.

> "As a person who has struggled with reading problems all of my life, I believe that people who learn differently look at the world from unique perspectives. Many of our students are highly creative, visualizing solutions that might not occur to the rest of us. By identifying what gets in the way of learning for students, we are able to nurture their strengths, improve their self-esteem, and teach them the skills they will need to become our inventors, leaders, and entrepreneurs.

> "As parents, clinicians, and teachers, we have the opportunity—and the responsibility—to positively influence our children's lives."

Charles Schwab didn't let dyslexia prevent him from succeeding in the world of finance. Happily, his success is turning out to be someone else's good fortune as well.

# ROBERT SHAPIRO

## "MEET YOUR GOALS, NOT SOMEONE ELSE'S"

Many lawyers do their jobs and never find themselves written up in every major newspaper and magazine in the country. But if you are Robert Shapiro, and you are a member of the defense team on what some have called "the trial of the century"—the O.J. Simpson trial—your days of being a relative unknown disappear for good.

Not that Robert Shapiro was unheard of before the big trial. After graduating from law school, he served as a deputy district attorney in Los Angeles before establishing a solo practice. He was named Best Criminal Defense Attorney by the Century City Bar Association a short time before he took the job that brought him to everyone's attention.

Given the outcome of the trial, you would assume that to an attorney like Robert Shapiro, success means winning every case. That's not what he said, however, when he wrote down his thoughts for us:

"Success is a state of mind, I think. The personal triumphs that one achieves as a result of his or her own efforts are many times more valuable than the accidental attainment of any prize.

"When we master a musical instrument or a foreign language, for example, we bask in the satisfaction of accomplishment. True success is an 'A' on a child's report card, an athlete's personal best, the will to break a bad habit.

"Success, to me, means winning my own approval—and happiness goes hand in hand with success."

Success, he is saying, is not about winning or losing. It's about setting your own standards for success, and working toward meeting or exceeding them. When you can look at the work you have done and say, "I accomplished what I set out to do," that is success.

# Socks, the First Cat

## "Practice Makes Purrfect"

I'm sorry to say that our First Cat was a little reticent about sharing his thoughts on success and happiness (although he did send a nice paw print and a postcard with a quote that said, "I am honored to be your First Cat"). And though I would never presume to speak for this illustrious feline, here is what I think Socks *might* say if he could (and if he would):

> "If you're a cat, be a cat—and be the best cat you can be. Don't try to be (shudder!) a dog, or anything other than what you are.

> "Because once you know who you are, then you can figure out what it is you want to do with your life (chase mice, wait for firemen/firepersons to rescue you from treetops, etc.). And once you know what you want to do, you

can study, observe, ask questions, acquire skills, and . . . practice, practice, practice until you're practically perfect at what you do.

"Wasn't it Ralph Waldo Emerson (no doubt a cat lover) who said, 'If a man make a better mouse-trap than his neighbor, though he build his house in the woods, the world will make a beaten path to his door'? I believe I've quoted him purr-fectly."

# THE STATLER BROTHERS

## "ALL WORK AND NO PLAY . . ."

They say, "It ain't braggin' if it's so," so the Statler Brothers aren't bragging when they say they have won more than 500 awards—more than any other act in the history of country music.

It's also not bragging to say that their television show is tops on The Nashville Network. Or that they've stayed true to their roots by choosing to go on living in their hometown of Staunton, Virginia.

Did I mention their sense of humor? There's the story (they call it a legend) of how they got their name. Originally called the Kingsmen, they were forced to choose another name when another group called the Kingsmen hit it big with the song, "Louie, Louie." They say they were sitting in a hotel room when Harold saw a tissue box with the brand name "Statler" printed on it. They knew there was also a hotel in New York called the

Statler, and the name sounded classy, so "Statler Brothers" it was. But as Harold pointed out, "We might have been called the Kleenex Brothers."

Country music seems to shift gears every few years. What's popular one day is out of vogue the next. Through it all, the Statlers—Harold Reid, Phil Balsley, Jimmy Fortune, and Don Reid—have managed not just to survive, but to thrive. When you read the letter they wrote to me, I think you'll see why.

> "Success and happiness are often two unrelated subjects but, thank God, in our case they have worked hand-in-hand for four very rewarding careers and fulfilling lives.
>
> "We learned very early on, over thirty years ago, that doing what we love to do—sing and entertain—would be the thing that would make us happy. To be successful at it would make us ecstatic. We also learned very early that happiness must always be the goal, never money.
>
> "Money is the reward, but if it ever becomes the goal, you will lose sight of your dream and do things that make no one happy.
>
> "When we were struggling and bringing home the bare essentials, we were still happy because

we were doing what we wanted to do with our lives. You must love what you want to do so much that you are willing to do it for nothing. Then you know you're doing it for the right reasons. Those years when we worked our day jobs and went out to sing every weekend and most weekday nights, and then got up every morning with just a couple hours of sleep and went back in to our jobs, were wonderful. You couldn't have told us that then, but we know now we were proving something to ourselves. We were building and dreaming and planning, and we were happy.

"Once success came, we learned another hard lesson. Work, no matter how rewarding, can consume your life and family if you allow it to do so. Everyone plans their work schedule and sets aside the days and hours they work—and then their free time, their fun time, their family time, is left to fate. Whatever time is left over, that's the leisure time.

"Well, that can make a young man old very fast. And you can turn around one day and find that your family has grown up and left you. So we have always planned our leisure time right along with our work time. 'This month we tour. This month we record. This month we do TV, and these months the kids are out of school, so we take off and play.' This formula has proven to work for us.

"Success and happiness can go perfectly together if you allow it to happen. If you make it happen."

# TED TURNER

## "LEND A HAND"

People thought Ted Turner was crazy when he proposed a 24-hour-a-day news channel. No one thinks that anymore. CNN *Headline News* has leapfrogged over the competition with its coverage of late-breaking news.

As owner of the Atlanta Braves baseball team and the creator of three other cable TV networks, Ted Turner is a man who has definitely made his mark in the world. I'm happy to say that he has also been a tremendous encouragement to all of us at the Narrative Television Network. As we were seeking to do something new and unique, it was nice to follow a trail that had been blazed by a true pioneer like Ted Turner. He was gracious enough to endorse my first book, *You Don't Have To Be Blind To See,* and I am glad to share part of a letter he wrote to me a short time after NTN went on the air.

"**Man should be judged by the deeds done to help his fellow man.**

"All of us have handicaps of one sort or another, and it is important that we lend a hand to each other so we can share the gifts we have been given.

"Regardless of how busy we get in our daily lives, we must take time out to identify areas and ways in which we can help others. Christmas is a common time for this, but people should give of themselves year-round."

This letter was written five days before Christmas—a time of year when most busy executives are not even in their offices, much less dictating letters to the new kid on the block. I would say that in writing this letter to us, and the letter he wrote two years later to congratulate us on winning our Emmy, Ted Turner was demonstrating that if you want to get ahead, you need to pay attention. You need to be aware of what others are doing, applaud their efforts, acknowledge their successes, and encourage them in their pursuits. When we all help one another, everybody wins.

# THE MOST REVEREND DESMOND M. TUTU

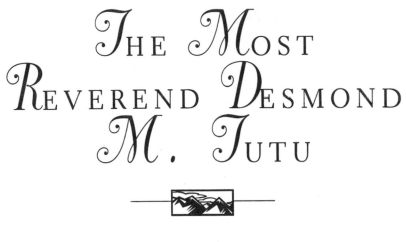

## "YOU ARE LOVED"

It takes courage to stand up for your beliefs. No one knows this better than Archbishop Tutu. It was in the late 1970s that this relatively unknown bishop moved to the front of the anti-apartheid movement in South Africa. Recommending economic sanctions against his country and other nonviolent means of change, he was highly deserving of the Nobel Peace Prize that was awarded to him in 1984. Apartheid in South Africa has all but disappeared as we face the 21st century. Despite his international fame, however, Archbishop Tutu hasn't lost sight of what's most important. He wrote to me:

> "So many of us suffer from the success/achievement/rat-race syndrome which says you matter only because you have made it. Most of

us think that this attitude carries over into our relationship with God, that God loves us because we are lovable, we deserve to be loved, and we have made it by impressing God. The truth, the Good News, is that God loves me. Period. That is the most fundamental truth about me, about you. It is a free gift, unearned, undeserved.

"God loves me not because I am lovable. I am lovable because God loves me. That is what gives me my worth and nothing can change it."

# Richard Valeriani

## "Defy the Odds"

In the news business, success is scooping all the other reporters. It's Woodward and Bernstein cracking Watergate. It's becoming a familiar face on the evening news. Or, at least, that is how it appears to those of us on the outside.

If you talk to correspondent Richard Valeriani, who spent a couple of decades in the news trenches at NBC, you will get a different story. In fact, you will get *someone else's* story. He had this to say:

> "At work, if you do what you want and you like what you do and you do it as well as you can, then you'll be successful, no matter what you do or how much you earn.
>
> "In life, happiness is obviously a state of mind —your state of mind. If you choose to be happy, you can be happy. Only you can make yourself unhappy.

"I heard an inspiring story recently about the associate choreographer for the Miss America Pageant.

"After he had auditioned for the job by dancing —and had been selected—he went to see the director of choreography. 'I have to tell you something,' he said. 'Don't worry,' she said, 'you have the job.' But he insisted: 'I have to tell you that I was born without legs.' The director gasped in disbelief, and when she had composed herself, she asked, 'If you were born without legs, then why in the world did you decide to become a dancer?'

"'Because,' he said, 'it was the one thing they said I could never do.'

"Always remember this: It's never easy."

You can say that again.

# $\mathcal{D}$ICK $\mathcal{V}$AN $\mathcal{P}$ATTEN

## "YOUR BEST IS ENOUGH"

I have run into Dick Van Patten at several celebrity/charity functions. He seems to turn up everywhere. But when you talk to the people who are really involved with community service work, you learn that he is much more than a figurehead, or a name on the program. He truly commits his time, energy, and talent to efforts he feels are important.

Mr. Van Patten was a mere child when he made his Broadway debut. He went on to do several more plays, a radio series and radio plays, more than a dozen movies, and a few television series. His signature role was Tom Bradford in *Eight Is Enough*.

I was lucky to catch up with Dick Van Patten as I gathered the material for this book. He was in Chicago, working on the play *Show Boat*. I'm glad he took the time to write me this brief note:

> "I have been in show business since the age of
> seven. Even though it is a very competitive
> business, and there is a great deal [to reflect on],
> I feel as long as you do the best you can and put

**in that little bit of extra work, all will come out
the way it is supposed to."**

You don't have to start your career in kindergarten if you want
to ensure your ultimate success. You only have to learn to go the
extra mile.

# $\mathcal{K}$EN $\mathcal{V}$ENTURI

## "BEAT THE HEAT"

O ne of my favorite weekend activities when I'm at home or traveling is enjoying a golf tournament on television. Since I am unable to see, the commentators are the most important aspect of the broadcast. Ken Venturi is my favorite. Not only is he a great commentator, he is a former champion who brings the same winning attitude to his work today.

Golf was not Ken Venturi's first career choice. He thought he would become a dentist and play golf for fun. Instead, he turned pro in 1956 and proceeded to have four outstanding years. In 1961, however, he hit a slump that made him the invisible man in professional golf.

Then came 1964. Suffering from heat exhaustion, he nonetheless managed to win the U.S. Open. For this inspiring feat, he was named "Sportsman of the Year" by *Sports Illustrated*, and PGA Player of the Year. End of the story? Not hardly. Shortly after his dramatic victory, he developed a rare circulatory and nerve ailment in his hands that forced him into surgery and therapy. Determination brought him back to the tour, where he regained his style and continued to play good golf for the rest of his career.

His new career, commentating, seems like a natural choice . . . unless you know that he had to overcome stuttering to make the grade. So, you see, some successes are hard-won.

When I asked Ken Venturi to contribute to this book, he sent me a lot of information about one of his favorite charities, Guiding Eyes for the Blind. It's an organization he has supported for many years. In fact, each year there's a Ken Venturi Guiding Eyes Classic, a golf charity benefit that raises funds to train guide dogs.

He also sent me a copy of an interview he did with *PGA Magazine*. It includes a story that tells a lot about this successful man's character.

When asked to name the best golf course he ever played, Ken Venturi said this:

> **"I would choose Cypress Point. I used to caddie there. The chefs used to help me out when I was a kid, and give me fried chicken . . . for lunch. . . . And the caddies would always help me out. I was just 14 or 15. And I never forgot that.**
>
> **"I went back there after having won the U.S. Open, and they all said, 'Ohhh, the big shot is**

here. The big boy. We thought you'd forget us now because you won the Open.'

"I said, 'Are you kidding me, you guys? Would I forget you?' And the caddies gathered around me while I opened the trunk of my car; I had brought a whole bunch of fried chicken. And I said, 'Now you can have lunch on me.' And I had also iced down some Dom Perignon. And the caddies and I sat there and had fried chicken and Dom Perignon."

Explaining why he returned to Cypress Point that day, Ken Venturi gave the credit to his father.

"When I told him I wanted to be somebody, he said, 'I will always pray that you will be somebody. But I will pray more that you never forget where you came from.'"

He proved that he has a good memory, and I believe he also has a good attitude about life. I think it's the key to his success. As he told PGA *Magazine*:

"I don't believe you have to be better than everybody else. I believe you have to be better than you ever thought you could be.

"I only lasted ten and a half years on the Tour. . . . I feel that, in that time, I did the very best I could."

That's all that any of us can do.

# Dr. Denis Waitley

## "Believe It... See It...Have It"

Few people have influenced my life like Dr. Denis Waitley. He has been a shining example of excellence his entire life.

As a Blue Angel pilot, through his work as a psychologist with the returning Vietnam POWs, and now as a best-selling author and a member of the Platform Speakers Hall of Fame, Dr. Waitley's message of hope has never changed. He encouraged me early on as a motivational speaker, and was the catalyst who got me started on my first book. (He wrote the foreword to *You Don't Have To Be Blind To See.*) We've shared a platform together and worked on television together, so I'm proud to include a few of his words of wisdom in this book. I agree wholeheartedly with his philosophy:

> "The world tells us not to believe it until you see it. I know that you'll see it when you believe it.

"You can envision a bigger and more personally fulfilling destiny for your life. And what you begin to see, you can begin to have."

What Dr. Waitley is telling us to do, in essence, is to get rid of that voice inside our heads that says, "I can't succeed," and replace it with a voice that says, "I *can* succeed and I *am* succeeding!" When you start to see yourself—in your mind—as you *can be*, as a success, it won't be long before the person you dream (and believe) you *can be* will emerge. Keep telling yourself that you have *already arrived*, and see if that doesn't inspire you to make that conviction a visible reality.

# Mort Walker

## "TURN YOUR BACK
## ON DEFEAT"

C an it be true that Beetle Bailey will turn 50 at the turn of the century? And that Hi and Lois won't be far behind him?

Unlike the rest of us, comic strip characters don't really age. And fortunately for us, comic strip creators such as Mort Walker seem to get better with age.

We would need another book to list all the awards that Mort Walker has earned. But you can put away the pedestal. This man is the working man's cartoonist. Take a look at the thoughts he shared with me, and see if you don't agree.

> "When I was very young, our family was very poor and I was very sorry for myself. Then I observed that almost everyone had problems . . . financial, physical, racial . . . all kinds of problems.
>
> "I decided that the only thing that defeats people is accepting defeat.

"I was determined that I was going to be a successful cartoonist and make some money. I wrote at the top of my drawing board, 'I will not be denied,' and I set out to work harder and climb farther than my competitors with the belief that hard work never killed anybody.

"It worked. I think people like to help people achieve their dreams. I had so many people do nice things for me, and I think they shared in the joy of my success. Success wasn't without some setbacks, but they provided some excitement in making me step back and analyze the problem and go on to try to win. And the thrill of winning is exhilarating.

"I've been labeled the 'incurable optimist' because I always believe I can make things work out. Sometimes they don't, but most times they do. And I firmly believe a positive attitude will get you farther than a negative one.

"I've played golf with blind people and had a great time. I've had dinner with people who had no arms and ate with their feet. I've done drawings in hospitals for soldiers who have no hope, and shared a laugh. There is something noble in accepting a bad deal and rising to the occasion with your head held high and a determined smile on it.

"Easy for me to say."

But Mort Walker doesn't just talk the talk; he walks the walk.

# JOSEPH WAMBAUGH

## "GO BELOW THE SURFACE"

Joseph Wambaugh was a police officer in Los Angeles for fourteen years. In the three years before he left the force, he published his first three novels. One of his best-known books, published in 1973, is *The Onion Field*; he received the Edgar Allan Poe Award from the Mystery Writers of America the following year.

Like many who contributed to this book, Joseph Wambaugh does not consider himself an expert on success. But I believe he makes a point that all of us would be wise to consider and incorporate into our daily lives:

> "The only thing I have learned about success is that if one is willing to listen, *really* listen, to things that are said, as well as to things that are *not* said, that person will be miles ahead of the competition.

"Many writers who handle English prose far better than I, never achieve their potential because they have never learned to listen; hence, they never truly understand the human heart."

# DR. RUTH
WESTHEIMER

## "DON'T JUDGE A BOOK
BY ITS COVER"

F ew people have ever known the recognition and notoriety
that has come to Dr. Ruth Westheimer. Nearly everyone
is aware of her books, and of her work on television and
radio. But few people know the real Dr. Ruth. We have had the
opportunity to work together at several conventions and press
conferences. She has always been a powerful encouragement to
me and to everyone around her.

I remember that, in 1991, a cable TV network announced
that Dr. Ruth would be handling some of their broadcasts from
the Democratic and Republican convention floors. She and I
were at a press conference the next day when an uninformed
reporter attacked her for getting involved in the broadcast of a
political convention. When he said that having Dr. Ruth do such
a broadcast would turn the entire election into a joke, Ruth
calmly responded:

"As someone who lost both of my parents in a concentration camp and grew up as an exiled prisoner myself, I think I understand the power and the value of a free society as well as anyone."

Dr. Ruth reminds all of us that the freedoms we have make everything possible. No matter what tragedies you've suffered in your personal life, you can rise above them and make your own place in the world.

# JAMES WHITMORE

## "TREASURE THE ADVENTURE"

In 1947, actor James Whitmore was named Most Promising Newcomer. It turned out to be a prophetic award. He has given a number of notable performances on Broadway, and his movie work has resulted in two Academy Award nominations. Some of you might remember him as the convict with the bird in his pocket in *The Shawshank Redemption*.

With half a century of work under his belt, James Whitmore can look back with pride on his contributions to the entertainment industry. This is what this gifted actor wrote when I asked him to talk about success and happiness:

> "After 75 years as an occupant of this planet Earth, I have only this to say:
>
> "Life is the most precious gift ever given.
>
> "It knows not of good or ill. If we treat it with love and respect, in ourselves and in others, it will return to us fulfillment.

"The American Indians said of it, 'Thou shall acknowledge the wonder.'

"Both life and death are part of the same great adventure."

As so many of the people in this book have said, it all comes down to attitude. If you believe the glass is half full, you are a lot more likely to succeed at whatever you try . . . and to find happiness in the process.

#  ANDY WILLIAMS

## "SURROUND YOURSELF
## WITH WHAT YOU LOVE"

A ndy Williams has become synonymous with the holiday season for millions of people around the world. I have been to his theatre in Branson, Missouri, on several occasions, and enjoyed his Christmas performance as a kick-off to our family's holiday celebration.

Long before he built his theatre, he built a reputation in the music business as a singer of love songs. His 17 gold albums, Emmy Awards, and Grammy Awards are appropriate honors for the man who gave us "Moon River," "Days of Wine and Roses," "Born Free," and the theme songs from the movies *Love Story* and *The Godfather*, among many others.

I had the opportunity to interview him in a beautiful apartment he has built right behind the stage of his (appropriately named) Moon River Theatre. I observed that, in much the same way that the holiday season is about gathering friends and family and things we care about around us, Mr. Williams has created a life for himself that emphasizes the things that are important to him and that bring him happiness, peace, and joy.

> "Happiness, I think, is really the most important thing."

He told me,

> "And I'm happy here in Branson. I've got a lovely wife, two wonderful dogs, a home that I like very much, and this theatre. And I live on a golf course, and I like to play golf. So I've got just about everything around me that I really love."

In the long run, success is not measured in dollars and cents. Money helps, but being at peace with yourself and with those you love is of much more value.

#  SHEB WOOLEY

## "FIND YOUR SLOT"

At a time when westerns ruled the airwaves, *Rawhide* was one of the best on television. (A little-known actor named Clint Eastwood used the show as a stepping-stone to big-screen stardom.)

Also appearing on *Rawhide* was an actor named Sheb Wooley. He stayed with the show for its first six years, then drifted out of sight before making a brief comeback on *Hee Haw*.

The experiences of actors like Sheb Wooley are proof that nothing lasts forever. The longest-running television shows must end. The best movies are soon supplanted by new ones. So when you create your own personal definition of success, keep in mind that what was success yesterday might not be tomorrow. By all means have short-term goals, but be sure to have a long view as well. Be grateful for those "15 minutes of fame" if they come your way, but don't feel like a failure once they're gone. Listen to Sheb Wooley's advice:

> **"I believe that each of us is created and led to
> serve a certain function in life. If we follow**

intuitive guidance (ask for it, listen for it), we will find our slot, and when we do, success is assured.

"Dreams want to come true. So dream the dream and go for it."

Fame is fleeting, but success can be yours if you just learn to recognize it when you have it.

# ＦAY ＷRAY

## "DON'T WASTE TIME COMPLAINING"

Fay Wray will always be best remembered for her role in the original *King Kong* movie. (You might say that her distinctive scream placed her head and shoulders above the crowd.) When the film was celebrating its 50th anniversary, I was happy to have a chance to sit down and interview her.

She shared with me an honest appraisal of her strengths and weaknesses—rather unusual for an actress. But as she talked, I realized once again that being able to take a critical look at yourself is crucial if you want to succeed. Fay Wray's ability to do so helped her "keep her head" in a business that's hard on the ego.

> "I know I was hired for many roles simply because of the way I looked. Being attractive can open many doors. But during my entire career, I fought to be taken seriously. I fought for serious roles.

"If there's one thing I have learned, it is that I don't believe in complaining.

"You simply do the best you can with what you've got, and somehow it works out."

Considering that she made more than 30 movies before *King Kong*, and more than 40 movies after, her formula must work.

# JANE WYATT

---

## "BELIEVE IN YOURSELF"

She played Mr. Spock's mother in *Star Trek IV: The Voyage Home,* but it was on television that Jane Wyatt set an unbeatable standard for motherhood. Her role on *Father Knows Best* earned her three Emmy Awards and the status of an icon.

At the time I interviewed her, I was struck by her comment that, in her own mind, she had always been certain of her success. When I went on to ask her what she would have done had she not become an actress, she stated, with total conviction:

> **"It never occurred to me to do anything else. And it never occurred to me that I would not be successful."**

This level of conviction teaches us that your level of belief can create a self-fulfilling prophecy in your life. This is why Jane Wyatt has enjoyed not only a tremendous career, but a fulfilling personal life as well. She *made* it happen.

# LORETTA YOUNG

## "PUT YOUR BEST FOOT FORWARD"

The Narrative Television Network has presented several movies featuring Loretta Young. There are literally dozens to choose from, including *The Farmer's Daughter,* for which she won an Academy Award in 1947. And it wasn't just the world of movies that she conquered. She won three Emmys for her 1950s TV series, and a Golden Globe Award in the late 1980s for a made-for-TV movie.

Beauty, grace, and style are what come to mind when you think about Loretta Young. She has always been a "movie star" in the truest sense of the words.

During an interview I did with her, she happily talked about some of the other great stars with whom she had worked in the past, including Edward G. Robinson, Cary Grant, and Orson Welles. Her vivid recollections allowed the audience to "meet" these stars who are no longer with us.

I wondered how she had managed to rise to the top of her profession, and to remain there for so many years. The comments she made gave a good indication of her character, and I think we can all learn something from her beliefs.

> "Never indulge in jealousy or envy. Those two destructive emotions will eat you alive."

> "A beautiful face gets you the first five minutes. After that, you're on your own."

> "Everything worthwhile, everything of any value, has a price. The price is effort."

> "An optimistic mind is a healthy mind."

> "Charm is simply this: the Golden Rule, good manners, good grooming, good humor, good sense, good habits, and a good outlook."

Anyone who lives by those rules deserves to succeed.

# ROBERT YOUNG

## "YOU HAVE TO HAVE ENTHUSIASM"

A ctors who have more than one successful long-running television series to their credit are a fairly exclusive group. (Harry Morgan, Bill Bixby, and Michael Landon come to mind.) But don't forget Robert Young, who made more than 80 movies before becoming the often-imitated, but-never-equaled patriarch on *Father Knows Best* in the late 1950s and early 1960s. Several years after the show completed its run, he was back in prime time with the beloved doctor, *Marcus Welby, M.D.*

Being an actor was not his goal, much less becoming a star. But once he had his foot in the door, there was no stopping him. I'll let him tell his story.

> "I really had not planned on becoming an actor. I had done some work in high school (*Robin Hood*), but after graduation I had taken a job in a brokerage house. I was at work

one day when my Lincoln High English teacher happened by. She wanted to know how my acting career was going. 'What career?' I answered. She put me in touch with my old drama teacher who sent me, with a glowing recommendation, to the Pasadena Playhouse.

"While at the Playhouse, I gained much valuable experience, but since I wasn't getting paid there, I hung on to my day job. At about this time, I chanced upon a book with the imposing title, *How to Become an Actor*. As I recall, the first paragraph of the book contained a line something like, 'The secret of becoming a successful actor is ENTHUSIASM.' This gave me both hope and purpose.

"I may not have had technique or even talent at that time, but, by heaven, if there was one thing I *did* have, it was ENTHUSIASM.

"My work became, I can truly say, both passion and pleasure for the next 60 years. I never lost my zest for it, but now, nearing 90, I feel I am entitled to a bit of a rest.

"By the way . . . these early events at the Playhouse took place around the time of the '29 market crash. About that time, acting started to look better and stocks a whole lot worse. Who knows? If it weren't for the Great Depression, I might never have gotten into the acting profession at all. You see, I lost my job at the brokerage house, and I HAD TO do something else."

Isn't it funny how, when we do what we have to do, it oftentimes turns into something that we love?

# CONCLUSION

You have just heard from some of the most creative minds and best-known achievers of our time. *Their* success should no longer separate you from them, but—to the extent you embrace their wisdom—should help you create *your* success.

It's very easy for you and me to read about famous people and believe in their past and even their future success. But the difficulty comes when we are faced with the prospect and the possibility of our own success. Winners believe that success exists for everyone, and that their success does not diminish anyone else's. Success, they believe, is available in an unlimited supply, like oxygen. They don't hesitate to breathe in all they want or need because for them, it's the natural thing to do. They assume that everyone will breathe in all the oxygen—or in this case, success—that they want, and that it in no way will diminish the infinite supply.

As you re-read this book and begin to embrace the principles that apply to your specific destiny, I want you to know that *I believe in your success*. This book was written for *you*. I don't believe that anyone who reads this book has had any more doubts and fears or has felt more inadequate than I have. Believing in my own success is a constant battle. It is the ultimate battle that we all face, which is the battle for the mind. It is the only real battle in the world.

I want you to know that, as you undertake your battle for belief, *I already believe in you.* Any time you feel that winners are different or special or set apart from the rest of us, and any time you feel that no one believes in you, simply pick up a phone and call (918) 627-1000, and ask to speak to me. Our phones are answered around the clock by real people, not computers. These people know that there is one kind of call I will always take or return promptly: a call from someone who has heard me speak or read my books. The people who answer our phones know that I will speak to anyone who is battling for belief. That's because I want you to know that in your moment of crisis, in your most difficult day, at your lowest point, *I will always believe in you and your success.*

I look forward to your success and to including your success secrets in a future book. Please do not deprive yourself, your family, or the world of your greatness. Mediocrity is the most selfish pursuit of any human being. *Your success* is the greatest gift that you can give to all of humanity.